HAPPINESS:

ISSUES OF EMOTIONAL LIVING
IN AN AGE OF STRESS
FOR CLERGY AND RELIGIOUS

THE SEVENTH
PSYCHOTHEOLOGICAL SYMPOSIUM

KATHLEEN E. KELLEY

RICHARD J. GILMARTIN

MARIE R. HOFER

J. WILLIAM HUBER

THOMAS A. KANE

VINCENT M. BILOTTA III

AUDREY CAMPBELL-WRAY

JOHN A. STRUZZO

EDITED BY THOMAS A. KANE

AFFIRMATION BOOKS
WHITINSVILLE, MASSACHUSETTS

All income derived from the sale of this book is used to provide care for priests and religious suffering from emotional unrest.

AFFIRMATION BOOKS is an important part of the ministry of the House of Affirmation, International Therapeutic Center for Clergy and Religious, founded by Sister Anna Polcino, S.C.M.M., M.D.

To
present and former residents
of the House of Affirmation
with love and gratitude

Published with Ecclesiastical Permission

First Edition

© 1982 by House of Affirmation, Inc.

Library of Congress Cataloging in Publication Data
Psychotheological Symposium, 7th, 1981, Fontbonne Academy,
etc.
  Happiness: issues of emotional living in an age of stress for
clergy and religious.
    1. Catholic Church—Clergy—Psychology—Congresses.
  2. Monastic and religious life—Psychology—Congresses.
  3. Happiness—Congresses. I. Kelley, Kathleen E. II. Kane,
Thomas A., 1940-   . III. Title.
  BX1912.7.P78 1981   253'.2   82-1733
  ISBN 0-89571-014-5   AACR2

Printed by
Mercantile Printing Company, Worcester, Massachusetts
United States of America

CONTENTS

Preface

As a boy I grew up not far from Plymouth Rock where the pilgrims first landed in America. They brought with them their Puritan religion, a significant influence in the formation of American idealism. Puritanism was once defined as the haunting fear that someone somewhere might be happy. I am not sure why, but something of this notion still keeps creeping into our understanding of religion: if you avoid happiness in this life, you will be happy in the next.

This was not the understanding of the great saints, and the founders of many religious congregations. In spite of suffering and unrest, they spoke of God's love, mercy, and joy. Francis of Assisi once described himself and his band of followers as "God's servants and his minstrels who must inspire the hearts of people and stir them to spiritual joy." At one of the darkest moments near the end of his life, as he lay afflicted with partial blindness and in pain from his sickness, Francis composed his great poem, "The Canticle to Brother Sun." It is one of the most glorious and joyful hymns praising the Creator ever written and is a classic of medieval literature.

For seven successive years House of Affirmation staff members have presented symposia on significant topics intended to help individuals work out their answers to life's questions. We do not pretend to have all the answers, but rather do we strive to provide reflections and challenges which individuals can use to create their own directions, to determine for themselves where they are going. We have addressed the issues holistically by using the best insights provided by reputable contemporary psychology accompanied by appropriate reflections from theology, religion, and scripture. Wherever possible we integrate these disciplines.

The theme of our seventh annual symposium was happiness. It presented us with the challenge to consider an area of concern so frequently either taken as obvious, or avoided by academic communities because it is ambiguous or threatening. I am proud of what my colleagues have written here to encourage your faith and challenge your thought.

As I now express gratitude to all who presented papers at the Boston, San Francisco, and St. Louis sessions of the 1981 symposium, I would also like to thank the audiences who attended the sessions. Each year they stimulate us indirectly as we consider what theme to address at the symposium, and how to develop the topics in a way that will help all the participants.

The symposium sessions could not have been held without a large supporting group of friends and staff members who donated their time and energies on the days involved: to each and all, I offer heartfelt gratitude. I am also grateful to those who extended hospitality for the meetings: the Sisters of St. Joseph at Fontbonne Academy in Milton, the Sisters of the Presentation in San Francisco, and the staff at St. John's Mercy Hospital in St. Louis.

In a world grown cold and gloomy because of universal contemporary problems of division, discord, violence, and mistrust, the Church and the world need a spirit of joy and optimism more than ever. Great men and women in Church history retaught their generations that the gospel is literally Good News, a living message of hope, happiness, and security in our loving Father's care. If we can live that spirit today, the Church will be well on its way to renewal and will be happy in the process. It is my hope that men and women will grow in happiness as the result of reading this book.

Thomas A. Kane, Ph.D., D.P.S.
Priest, Diocese of Worcester
Publisher, Affirmation Books
January 7, 1982   Whitinsville, Massachusetts

Sister Kathleen E. Kelley, S.N.D., M.Ed., is director of the House of Affirmation in Webster Groves, Missouri. A member of the Boston Province of the Sisters of Notre Dame de Namur, Sister Kelley received her undergraduate education at Emmanuel College in Boston and did graduate work in counseling at Boston College. Before joining the staff of the House of Affirmation, she served on her province administration team and held the position of province personnel director. Sister Kelley did career counseling at the House of Affirmation in Whitinsville before her appointment as director of the Webster Groves residential center. She has lectured extensively in the areas of mental health and the religious life in the United States and abroad.

"Happily Ever After"

Kathleen E. Kelley

Happiness may not be talked about often or directly, yet it concerns us all. It is elusive to many and it is known by its absence in some lives.

It has been the theme of philosophers and writers through the centuries. It was a concept important enough to be included in the Declaration of Independence, where Thomas Jefferson proclaimed that each person has the right to life, liberty, and the pursuit of happiness.

Happiness has even been studied scientifically in an effort to ascertain whether there is a formula for it.[1] Such a formula did not emerge, however. The results included some familiar statements: not all rich people are happy; not all rich people are unhappy. The study verified that not all poor people are happy and that not all poor people are unhappy. Money, sex, and power are elements of happiness for some and not for others. Most of the external circumstances of life and possessions were not considered major contributors to happiness. What did emerge as significant contributing factors to happiness were, interestingly enough, the vital elements of the Christian life: religious, spiritual, and ethical values; a sense of personal fulfillment; life goals; challenging work; and the most important element, love.

1. Jonathon Freedman, *Happy People* (New York: Ballantine Books, 1978).

Taken together, these elements suggest that happiness flows from a person's responsible involvement in and commitment to life. Happiness arises as a byproduct of living. The experience of happiness is different from simply "feeling good." A person can feel good on drugs but can hardly be called happy. "Highs," thrills, and excitement do not produce happiness. A happy person can enjoy these experiences, but they do not make a man or woman happy.

Happiness

Happiness is more the fundamental and abiding effect of a good life and a satisfying lifestyle rather than the experience of transitory peak moments. It is also a subjective experience, a feeling within a person whose life is in order. In such a life, goals have been attained or are attainable and personal values are being lived out in the context of responsible living. Happiness flows from a life of purpose, especially one that is ordered to the service of others. It is bound up with effort and discipline.

The gospel message that the person who is ready to lose his or her life truly finds it is fundamental to the achievement of any real happiness. Finally, happiness is associated with struggle rather than with achievement.

Unhappiness

It would seem, then, that since we have some notion of the prerequisites of happiness, the experience would be easily accessible to all of us. Yet one does not have to look far to see the faces of unhappy people. Eric Fromm remarked that our kind of "pursuit of happiness" does not produce well-being. He observed that "we are a society of notoriously unhappy people; lonely, anxious, depressed, destructive, dependent people who are glad when we have killed the time we are trying so hard to save."[2]

---

2. Erich Fromm, *To Have or To Be* (New York: Bantam Books, 1976), p. xxvii.

Americans, it is reported, spend more than one billion dollars annually on tranquilizers, sometimes called "happiness pills," to free them from anxiety and tension.[3] Thus it is evident that the experience of happiness is not a byproduct of living for some people. There are many unhappy persons who do not have goals or values out of which they shape their lives, who live in uncertainty, confusion, and anxiety.

Again there is evidence that one's life circumstances do not mark the dividing line between happiness and unhappiness. Some individuals with painful family backgrounds are happy. People with great personal handicaps, enduring constant pain, are happy. Someone who has all of life's goods may be miserable.

Since the objective aspects of life—one's circumstances, health, wealth, power—do not guarantee happiness, it would lead one to consider whether the subjective aspects are the key factors. These aspects are most fundamentally the way an individual relates to, copes with, and finally comes to an acceptance of reality.

I would like to explore this relationship between one's attitude toward reality and one's experience of unhappiness and happiness. The basis for the exploration is the belief that the promise of living "happily ever after" is fulfilled in living the message of Jesus in this moment of life.

Happily Ever After

The theme of this article emerged out of some recent history—the royal wedding in England. The media coverage showed a nation caught up in fantasy, despite the crises in the country—unemployment, civil strife, and chaos. Broadcasters repeatedly told the story as "once upon a time," they would live "happily ever after." The event seemed to captivate the British people and to give them a break from the harsh realities of life and from the routine of living. It likewise seemed to touch the child in persons

---

3. Arthur Gordon, "Happiness Doesn't Come in Pills," in *The Art of Living* (New York: Reader's Digest, 1980).

who long for a bit of Camelot, who consider happiness as unrelated to reality but to be found in fantasy. This wedding touched in people recollections of their own "once upon a time" memories, which most often are happy ones. There is something about recalling the past that minimizes the struggle that was present and focuses on the dream quality. There is often a sense of nostalgia associated with the past. The same sense of a dream quality is connected with the future, where men and women are convinced that happiness will be found. Past and future effectively block the only place where happiness can be experienced— the now moment of reality.

Memories of Happiness

The now moment of reality pales for most individuals when they recall their past happiness. Childhood is often remembered as a happy time, when people felt carefree and taken care of. Because this part of their life seemed "happy," some persons still view life from the perspective of their childish experiences, in hopes of recapturing them. Their attitude toward the present reflects their desire to recapture childhood: they want to be protected and secure, with no anxieties or pressures.

Paul speaks of his transition from childhood to adulthood: "When I was a child, I used to talk like a child and think like a child and argue like a child. But now I am a man, all childish ways are put behind me" (1 Cor. 13:11-12). In most people's lives, the transition is not so clear. Ideally, childhood expectations and attitudes are gradually modified as one replaces illusions about life with the experiences of the realities of life. Childhood fantasies that began "once upon a time" and ended "happily ever after" become the adult reality of dealing with the uncertainties and demands of living.

If responsibility for one's life and healthy independence are not dealt with and accepted, childish attitudes permeate one's living of life. Unhappiness for some men and women may result from the inability to let go of childhood myths. Their expectation that life should take care of them brings them into harsh conflict with the truth of reality. Attitudes that the world owes them, that life is unfair, that the childhood promise of living happily ever after has been unfulfilled, become blocks in dealing with truth and reality.

An individual who carries childish expectations and attitudes has great difficulty in coping with adult realities. Such people are unable to own their responsibility for their lives. They experience a sense of alienation from themselves and the world, feeling that the world they live in now is not the world they understood it to be from childhood experiences. There is a sense that life without illusions would be unbearable, yet living the illusions creates terrible anxiety.[4] Their efforts to block out, distort, change, and ultimately deny reality consume their energies. The result is a life of confusion, anxiety, and withdrawal from the arduous work of living. These people relate passively and a bit hopelessly to life.

Others face reality head on, but they do so filled with personal illusions. The childhood "once upon a time" stories of Robin Hood and Don Quixote and his impossible dream get lived out in contemporary dress. Such people ignore the realities of human limits and commit unlimited energies to unlimited involvements. They strive to overcome all evils, and although they may accomplish things, they do not attain a sense of personal wholeness and happiness. Their lives are marked by constant battles with reality rather than an acceptance and living-out of it. The truth of who they are gets lost in the myths of unreality.

The histories of some clergy, religious, and apostolic ministers present a possible parallel. They came into a system where they were taken care of and ensured freedom from ordinary worries, where decision making and responsibilities were limited. The changes came and illusions were shattered, leaving some persons angry and bitter, unable to cope well, alienated, and without a sense of belonging. Others recalled the "old days" of security with nostalgia. These men and women were not experienced in dealing with adult realities. The world they bought into was not

---

4. Sheldon Kopp, *An End to Innocence* (New York: Bantam Books, 1978).

the world they ended up living in, and the result for some was genuine unhappiness and disillusionment. They experienced a sense of disconnectedness with the world and a lack of self-knowledge. "Happily ever after" grew into "hopelessly ever after," a waiting life out, holding on to a promise in the next life through a willingness to endure misery in this one.

An individual who lives out of memories of the past and hopes of the hereafter misses the only chance that human beings have for happiness: the reality of the present, the now moment.

Happiness and Reality

The reality of now is the best starting point for happiness. It has been accurately commented that "if God created this world only as a temporary place of trial, he seems to have taken a wholly unnecessary amount of trouble in its construction."[5]

There must be something good here. If we do consider unhappiness as alienation from and rejection of reality, then happiness can be linked to a person's ability to accept, cope with, and relate out of reality. Reality means living with things as they are, not as they should be; living with the world as it is according to the way one is. Happiness is possible only in a context and the context is life's realities.[6]

However, life's realities are tough. The world is filled with suffering, war, injustices. Individuals face tragedies and suffering. We are limited people.

Facing self in the world as a human being means transforming childish attitudes and childish expectations into adult acceptance. "Take care of me" is changed into "I will take care of myself and reach out to others." No responsibility becomes an acceptance of responsibility. The denial of pressures and anxieties becomes an acceptance of them as part of life. Total security yields to a willingness to live with insecurity.

---

5. Alan W. Watts, *The Meaning of Happiness* (New York: Harper Colophon Books, 1968), p. 52.

6. Joseph B. Fabry, *The Pursuit of Meaning* (Boston: Beacon Press, 1968).

Personal Realities

On a personal level, reality means an acceptance of who I am: sinful yet graced, limited yet gifted. It means moving from "I wish I were" to "I am who I am." It means living out of the reality of limitations. I cannot fight all injustices, but I can fight some. It means a realization that perfection is not of this life; that the ideal is not the real. It means accepting active responsibility for my involvement in this world. An unhappy person is passive, feeling that life should give something to him or her. A happy person is actively in relationship to life and takes control of his or her individual life.

The extraordinary story of the Elephant Man highlights this distinction between unhappiness and happiness. He was faced with the tragedy of his reality; happiness came through accepting it and relating out of it.

Connecting with self on a human level and accepting the realities of self are the basis of coping with life and relating in truth to it. Self-knowledge is indispensable to an understanding of happiness. Persons who know and accept self will not set goals that are either beyond or beneath them. Rather, they will use personal strengths in a realistic approach to life and neither demand what can never be achieved nor turn away from what can be accomplished.[7]

These realizations of personal realities are intimately connected with spiritual realities. Scientific study has supported the idea that the key to happiness is in love and relationship. Christianity gives focus and meaning to that love. The promise of Christianity is one of living happily ever after, but happiness in the next life has to be earned in this one.

Paul writes to the Philippians: "I want you to be happy, always happy in the Lord. I repeat, what I want is your happiness." He continues, with an awareness of human concerns: "There is no need to worry. Present your needs to God . . . and that peace of

---

7. Eugene C. Kennedy, *The Pain of Being Human* (Garden City, N.Y.: Image Books, 1972).

God which is so much greater than we can understand, will guard your hearts and your thoughts" (Phil. 4:4-9).

The promise of Christianity is not a promise of life without pain or suffering but a pledge that we will not be overwhelmed. "You have in you the strength based on his own glorious power never to give in but to bear anything joyfully" (Col. 1:11-12). The promise was fulfilled through Jesus, who although he was divine, emptied himself to assume the condition of a slave.

Jesus took on limited humanity to show that it is possible for us, by living in this world and accepting our limitations, primarily through loving one another, to move toward the Resurrection and Happily Ever After.

Loving one another, in service to one another, is the most direct involvement in reality, because it faces us with the truth of who we are and calls us out of ourselves to relationships with others.

Between the Incarnation, recalled by many in the birthday celebration which enkindles the warmth of the memories of childhood past, and the Resurrection, the anticipation of a future happily ever after, comes life. Life faces us with personal crucifixions that are inherent in reality and offers us our only chance for a taste of happiness.

Happiness is connected with effort and struggle because it is connected with reality. Involvement with one another in the realities of the truth of who we are inevitably brings sacrifice and pain.

Reality means accepting the truth of who we are and living out that truth with and for one another, giving ourselves to others with a willingness to face the pains and problems of life. Scripture repeatedly confirms this: "There is no greater love than this: to lay down one's life for one's friends" (John 15:13-14). "Let us love in deed and in truth and not merely talk about it. This is our way of knowing we are committed to the truth and are at peace before him" (1 John 3:18-19).

For human realities to be imbued with these spiritual realities requires the discipline of prayer and reflection. The Lord is our bonding between the Incarnation and the Resurrection. To experience the joy of his abiding presence and to allow him to dwell in our hearts provide the strength to risk active involvement in life with one another.

Happiness is the byproduct of this immersion in life—one's own and others. It is the condition for following Christ when he said: "If anyone wants to be a follower of mine, let him renounce himself, and take up his cross every day and follow me. For anyone who wants to save his life will lose it but anyone who loses his life for my sake, that person will save it" (Luke 9:24-25).

Happiness, then, comes down to the difficult task of living in truth and loving one another. These relationships of truth and love, with ourselves and one another, force us to confront human limitations, the shadows within us, darkness, and untruths. They strip away the fantasies of "once upon a time."

The essence of happiness lies in the giving of ourselves and doing the right thing with our lives. It belongs to those who continue to work at loving despite disappointments and discouragements. But the promise of Jesus abides: "In the world you will have trouble, but be brave. I have conquered the world" (John 16:33).

Happiness is not free. The price is accepting responsibility for life. And the surest route to happiness is involvement in the Incarnation. That involvement breaks the myths and illusions about life, and faces us with the truth that "happily ever after" comes to those who pursue happiness through the reality of living.

Richard J. Gilmartin, M.A., P.D., is assistant director and full-time psychotherapist at the House of Affirmation in Whitins-ville, Massachusetts, and an associate professor of counseling psychology at Worcester State College and Anna Maria College. He received his graduate education at Fordham University, New York University, and St. John's University. Before joining the staff of the House of Affirmation he was psychological counselor at Worcester State College; director of counseling and instructor in the Graduate School at Assumption College, Worcester; chairperson of the psychology department at St. Francis College in Brooklyn; and supervising psychologist at the Religious Consultation Center of the diocese of Brooklyn.

Happiness and Development
in Middle Age

Richard J. Gilmartin

Man is a creature of hope: it is part of his better nature.
Xenophanes

The terms "happiness" and "middle age" in the title of this chapter are both strikingly vague. Before we can meaningfully address ourselves to the topic a clarification of these terms is in order.

Happiness

"Happiness," like a Rorschach inkblot, has different meanings for different people. What does it mean "to be happy"? We all think we know what happiness is, or at least know when we have it, or possibly, when we do not have it, but do we really? Would we agree on what it is to be happy, or even what it is to be unhappy? Or, is it such a subjective experience that it is non-communicable?

Many philosophers address themselves to the issue of happiness as a goal of human endeavor or as a byproduct achieved in some other pursuit. But we are hard pressed to find consensus among these same philosophers about what constitutes happiness. Advertisers promise us happiness if only we use their product. Although frequently subtle, the message is the same: happiness will be ours if only we use this deodorant, or brush with that toothpaste, or drive this car, or wear that pair of jeans. We are promised it, but rarely is it delivered.

Some tell us that sex brings happiness, others point to money, and still others say it can be found in religion. Some people seek happiness through sacrifice, others through indulgence. Some marry to find happiness, others divorce seeking the same happiness. Some point to power as the means to happiness, others state it can be found only in surrender and the refusal to have power. Most people enter psychotherapy in the search for happiness after other methods have failed.

The search for happiness is all around us and continues endlessly. Nevertheless, the question remains, "What is happiness?" Do we really know when we have it, or when we do not? Do we know the difference between being unhappy and being depressed, or discouraged, or ill? Do we know the difference between being happy and being elated, or successful, or healthy?

The concept of happiness is a difficult one for psychologists to work with, precisely because of its imprecision. Etymologically the word is interesting. It comes from the Old Norse word "happ," which literally translated means "good luck." Perhaps that is as precise as we can get. Being happy is a result of chance or luck. To be happy is to be lucky. It is not something that one can work for, or take responsibility for, but rather it is a result of fate, or kismet, or the spin of the wheel of fortune. The problem remains, however, because luck is not an easily explored concept.

I would suggest that a better word to work with than "happiness" is "peace." As a psychologist, I can have more to say about being at peace than I can about being happy. Peace is also a much more Christian term, one that is an integral part of our tradition. There is a long history of wishing each other peace as part of our liturgical expressions.

Peace has both an individual and a more global expression. There is peace between nations, as well as peace within oneself. By definition peace means being in harmony (with oneself), the absence of strife (within oneself), and being content (with oneself). To achieve peace is something we can do, both individually and, we hope, universally. I can make peace—I cannot make happiness.

Thus, what I am referring to is being at peace within oneself. To my mind, our topic should read: "Finding Peace in the Developmental Tasks of Middle Age."

Middle Age

We also need to examine more closely the term "middle age." It is unfortunate that the term generally has a pejorative meaning in our culture. To look "middle-aged" (except for the elderly) is not generally regarded as a compliment because our culture sees aging as a negative. Look at our advertisements and the age of those depicted: it is rare that one sees a middle-aged or elderly figure there. Our culture identifies attractive and desirable qualities with youth. The American people spend billions of dollars each year to disguise signs of their aging. Perhaps rightfully, some of us cry out against spending billions of dollars for military armaments while people are starving to death for lack of money to buy food. Should we not also decry the spending of billions of dollars on cosmetics that make us look young, while others are dying for lack of food? We who regard ourselves as counterculture people should also object to the prejudicial attitude of our society against aging.

When I was a graduate student, courses in developmental psychology typically were limited to child and adolescent psychology. Perhaps there were subcourses under these two, but it was generally held that human development began at conception and ended somewhere between the ages of nineteen and twenty-five, when growth "stopped." Reflective of this assumption were some of the theories of intelligence, especially as shown in such IQ tests as the Otis. In this test and similar ones where age norms are used, the raw score needed to achieve a certain IQ peaked in the late teens, remained stable in the twenties, began to decline in the thirties, and continued to decline after that. It was as if intelligence reached its peak in the late teens and remained relatively stable until the mid-thirties, when it began to decline.

We now know that this is not true and that scores on IQ tests will, within limits, continue to increase as long as one continues to exercise those abilities that the IQ test is measuring. Nevertheless, the belief that psychological growth parallels physical growth in accordance with a peak-plateau-decline paradigm is still very much with us.

This growth-decline concept is given poetic expression in that old Irish aphorism, "Man is twenty years growing, twenty years living, twenty years dying." This view of psychological growth as stopping at a certain age finds theoretical support in such instinct theorists as Sigmund Freud and Harry Stack Sullivan.

What I would like to suggest, however, is that just because we see the peak-plateau-decline growth paradigm in the physiological sphere, does not mean that it occurs in the psychological realm. Rather, I would suggest that nonphysiological growth is a lifelong and perhaps eternal process.[1] This concept may be what Elizabeth Kübler-Ross is conveying in the title of her recent book *Death: The Final Stage of Growth.*

Past is always prologue to future and the future continues to stretch out before us. A person of twenty-one has his or her entire life ahead. So too does a person of sixty-five. The latter may have fewer years, but the potential for growth is the same. All of life is growth, a continuous becoming.

There is an increasing interest in the stages of growth that occur after physical maturity is reached. I say stages because growth is best seen as steps in the mastery of successive developmental tasks necessary for continuing growth in a positive direction. Failure in the mastery of a particular developmental task means failure to reach a growth plateau, and thus the inability to address the next task. This failure appears to result in a unique depression called alienation. However, this alienation is not institutional, but personal; one feels alienated from oneself. The self becomes a stranger with whom I do not feel at home. I experience dullness, apathy, nondirected anger, and a longing to

---

1. For a more comprehensive discussion of growth as a lifelong process, see Theodore Lidz, *The Person* (New York: Basic Books, 1968).

escape into a nirvanalike fantasized existence. Life becomes a dull, meaningless chore: a burden that offers no respite except the tantalizing escape of alcohol or television. Our choice is growth or depression.

Before I focus on the developmental tasks of adulthood, I would like to return to the concept of "middle age." Since World War II, our culture has become increasingly youth oriented. Those personal qualities that we admire, value, and would most like to possess tend to be characteristic of early adulthood. The "ideal age" is seen as the mid-twenties. Those younger than that aspire to be seen as older, and those older aspire to seem younger. However, we may be on the verge of seeing a shift in this attitude.

The social prophet Alvin Toffler in his book *The Third Wave* predicts a switch from a youth-oriented culture to an aged-oriented culture. Sheer numbers are going to force this change. The fastest growing segment of our population is made up of those who are middle-aged or older. A look at a few statistics will help us to understand the implications of this trend.

In 1850 the mean life expectancy for men and women in the United States was forty. By the turn of the century the mean for men had risen to forty-eight and for women, to fifty-one. In 1975 it was sixty-seven for men and seventy-four for women. More and more people are moving into middle age and are forcing us to become aware of life after twenty-five.

What is "middle age"? There is anything but general agreement when one tries to put chronological limits on youth, middle age, and old age. Some define middle age as twenty-five to thirty-five, others as thirty-five to sixty. In some states people are eligible for elderly assistance at forty-five; in others, at sixty-five. Socially we generally begin the process of disengagement, which is a characteristic of old age, at sixty-five. Many persons, however, are actively nondisengaged well beyond this age. At best, defining "middle age" in chronological terms is arbitrary. If pressed, I would define middle age chronologically as twenty-five to eighty. A better definition would be that middle age is from the time one perceives oneself to be an adult (and is supported by others in this perception) to the time one begins the process of disengagement from active adulthood.

What should concern us more is that our culture has a negative attitude toward aging. It is important that we do not buy into and perpetuate that prejudice. As Anne Morrow Lindberg once said: "We tend to belittle the afternoon of life." One characteristic of the utilitarian orientation of our culture is a devaluation of aging. Other cultures, for example, some Oriental ones, accord status and prestige to the aged. But perhaps the very tendency to identify people in terms of age categories is itself destructive. Rather, life should be seen as an uninterrupted process, continuous growth, an ongoing confrontation with the tasks of living and growing. Perhaps this growth is an eternal process. We are forever beings in the process of becoming.

The greatest danger that we face is surrender to aging and death. Obviously there are physical changes that accompany the aging process, and these may place some limitations on us. But, at the same time, new adventures, new experiences, and new opportunities open up for us that were not available to us when we were younger. Life must be approached in search of these possibilities. To paraphrase a poet, I am not going to be happy in September by always wishing it were May.

This is where the achievement of a sense of peace lies. To be at peace is to be in consonance with my own life. It means that I am not warring with myself, not struggling or wrestling with myself to make myself something different from what my own humanness has made me. It means I am coping with my life, meeting and growing through its ongoing crises.[2] It gives me a sense of peace to know that I am in the flow of my life, continually

---

2. I use "crises" in the sense of turning points rather than catastrophic events. The Greek word "krisis" means a turning point wherein one is called "to decide." The crises I refer to here are the turning points of our lives at which we make decisions, either implicitly or explicitly, as to the direction we want to take ourselves.

changing (that is, turning) and growing, never arriving but always in process. I am never the learned one, but always a learner.

Tasks of Adulthood

There are many ways of looking at adulthood and many schemas of its developmental tasks. For my purposes here, the best approach to use is that of Erik Erikson. Although it is certainly not intended to be an exhaustive treatment of adult development, it is a comprehensive general model and one with which many are already familiar. It also lends itself to looking at issues in the life of the religious professional.[3]

Erikson sees as the final task of adolescence the achieving of a stable identity. But this is by no means completed as one enters adulthood. It will continue to evolve throughout one's life and may be radically altered at certain crisis points. In order to understand this process, we must examine the development of a person's sense of self and values.

Children find their sense of self and self-worth in their families. If asked to talk about themselves, preadolescents will describe themselves in a way that defines them as members of a family unit. Their sense of significance derives from the perceived significance of their family.

At adolescence a shift in the locus of identity takes place. Adolescents start to pull away from the family and to derive their sense of significance from peers. The adoption of the clothing, cosmetic styles, language, and music that identify one as a part of the adolescent subculture serves to reinforce the sense of separation from the family. In middle to late adolescence there is

---

3. I am using Erikson's work only as a schema and am not studying or commenting on Erikson's thoughts themselves. For a more detailed study of Erikson, see Robert Coles, *Erik Erikson: The Growth of His Work* (Boston: Little, Brown, 1970), or Erik Erikson, *Gandhi's Truth* (New York: Norton, 1969).

sometimes a further shift from peer identity to institutional identity. In the latter, one derives a sense of significance from the institutions with which one is affiliated.

As people enter adulthood, their work or profession provides a sense of significance or value.[4] If asked to talk about themselves, average adults will begin by saying what it is that they do for a living. For most of us, our self-description changes only as our work role changes. Middle adulthood may involve a reassessment of this identity, a fact that may be the basis of the so-called middle-age crisis.[5] Vatican II caused an upheaval in the previously stable identity of the priest or religious, and many were left with little sense of "who they were" or "what they were all about." It was the "middle-aged" priest or religious who was most affected by this uncertainty and most likely to search elsewhere for an identity.

Optimally there is yet another stage to this process, when we find meaning and value internally rather than in our work. This is probably only rarely totally achieved. Rather, varying amounts of significance are found in work and self: we increasingly derive a sense of satisfaction and value from the self we are becoming, but we still need the ego enhancement derived from knowing that we are effective and productive in our work. To derive one's sense of value totally from one's being is an ideal that is good to strive for but rarely achieved.

---

4. It has been postulated that adult males find their sense of significance in their work and that adult females find theirs vicariously through the work or social position of their spouse. It has also been suggested that adult males find significance in achievement, whereas adult females find it in intimacy. Both hypotheses appear too simplistic and probably represent cultural expectations rather than sex-linked realities. Both males and females are capable of finding significance in work achievement. It is also probable that intimacies are an ego-enhancing experience for both men and women.

5. The term "middlescence" was coined to describe this "crisis," thus showing its similarity to the "adolescent crisis."

Thus the achievement of a stable identity is a work that begins in preadolescence and continues throughout life. Calling it a "task of adolescence" does not mean that it is achieved prior to adulthood.

Erikson describes three main goals of adulthood and presents them in the order in which we confront them. They are best seen as choices (à la crises) that we make with regard to life, choices by which we enhance or inhibit the growth process.

Intimacy versus Isolation

Erikson conceptualizes the intimacy-versus-isolation stage as belonging to early adulthood, that is, late adolescence to early thirties. When a stable sense of identity is achieved, a man or woman can become involved with other people without fear of losing self-identity. He or she is not frightened by intimacy and is able to enter into intense personal relationships. Without this strong mutuality, be it in friendship or marriage, a sense of isolation grows to dangerous proportions and a life of exclusive self-interest or self-indulgence is pursued as a nongrowth-producing substitute.

Love and religion are the only means we have of assuaging our essential aloneness and isolation, and the fullest response to life requires that we embrace both. Religion without intimacy is meaningless ritual: at the very heart of the Christian life is the call to intimacy, with other persons as well as the Other.

It is unfortunate that we make "being intimate" synonymous with genitality, for the two are vastly different. Intimacy has much more to do with friendship than it does with a genital relationship. Perhaps one could define maturity as the ability to develop fruitful, loving relationships with other people on equal terms without being dominated or domineering.

But intimate relationships are not easy to make and maintain. They must be worked at. Intimacy does involve a loss of my personal freedom. When I enter into an intimate relationship it is as if I give away a piece of myself as a hostage. For those of us who value freedom and independence so highly this kind of giving can constitute a threat to our autonomy. But the giving is necessary if we are to continue to grow as persons.

It also takes effort to sustain an intimate relationship. We all enter relationships with expectations, and frequently these expectations are determined by our early life experiences. For example, expectations of being nurtured and being the object of the other's total concern are not uncommon in relationships. We must be able to sustain the disappointment, frustration, and anger that result from not having these expectations met. It is only when we stay with the relationship at such times that we are able to work through our unrealistic expectations and be open to experiencing the other as he or she is rather than through the prism of our expectations.

We should be wary of cheap, that is, instantaneous, intimacies; they frequently will be gone as quickly as they formed. Genuine intimacies take both time and effort. One of the commentators on the Talmud speaks of choosing someone to be a friend and then working so that he makes me his friend.

Generativity versus Stagnation

Erikson sees the stage of generativity versus stagnation as coming during the middle decades of adulthood. Choosing to be generative is not necessarily related to producing children but has more to do with making a contribution to the generations yet to come. The choice of stagnation means living to satisfy personal needs; to acquire comforts and entertainments for oneself; to engage in a self-absorbed lifestyle. Thus, in the growth process not only do "children" need "adults," but "adults" need "children."

Being generative does not mean being exclusively child oriented. The scientist in the laboratory can be just as generative as the teacher in the classroom. Whenever one is vitally involved in making life better for someone, there is generativity. It finds expression in a concern for the world one is leaving to future generations.

work *Sincerity and Authenticity.*[7] He sees authenticity as the result of sincerity. One chooses to be sincere, and it is through this choice that the authentic self emerges. It is interesting to note that the wish to seem sincere is the opposite of sincerity. To be sincere is the choice.

Sincerity and its resultant authenticity are requisite characteristics of the moral person. Although long recognized as a desirable personal characteristic, sincerity was not perceived as part of a moral life until approximately three hundred years ago. Sincerity became a morally significant issue when "man" began a search for his "true self" as opposed to his "socialized self." The process of socialization, albeit necessary, tends to distort the "true" or "natural" self. Through the work of philosophers, poets, and theologians we became aware of the destructive aspect of the socialization process. It is from this awareness that sincerity arose as an ethical requirement for Western civilization.

Children, because of their closeness to their instinctual life, may actually be more sincere (and thereby more authentic) than adults. The process of socialization can distance us from our inner self, and we thus need to resocialize ourselves to achieve authenticity. The biblical injunction to "become as little children" may have more to say on the issue of sincerity-authenticity than on simplicity of lifestyle.

Conclusion

Peace lies in being in the flow of one's own life—to face the tasks of growth and to continue to grow, without ever feeling that I have finally reached "it," because we are constantly called farther. Peace is found in growing as a person, psychologically and spiritually. One is alive only when he or she is growing. One becomes old when the process of disengagement from growing and changing begins.

---

7. Lionel Trilling, *Sincerity and Authenticity* (Cambridge, Mass.: Harvard University Press, 1972).

Peace is found in the challenge of intimacy, the call to generativity, and the triumph of integrity.

This sense of peace-in-becoming was captured for me in an article published in the *Personnel and Guidance Journal* by one of the pioneers in the counseling psychology movement in the United States, C. Gilbert Wrenn. This article was published shortly after Wrenn's retirement as Professor of Counseling Psychology at Arizona State University (Tempe). Wrenn writes:

> Does it seem bizarre to you that I, at age 73, *have* a future? Currently I talk to groups, attend boards and commissions, write, listen to others, love others. This is what I have been doing all of my life. . . .
>
> Someday, soon perhaps, some ailment will attack my body and it will be unable to fight back hard enough. I, as I am known to others, will have ceased to exist. . . . Is there a future for me beyond the time when the energy of my physical self is stifled and my body becomes ashes?
>
> I think there is a future for me. I do not fear Death, for it affects only the death of my body. . . . Life in my present state of existence has always been an adventure—loving, seeking, finding fulfillment in part and then finding new goals to beckon me on. After the death of my body, the excitement will surely not be gone; it may increase. I take with me into my new existence all that I have become, and I will perhaps find a freer chance to become even more.
>
> Of course, I know nothing of this life-beyond-the-body, but I have no fear of it, only a tingling anticipation. A few dear ones, in my family and out, will grieve as though I were gone. . . . If they could share with me the conviction that the "I" that they knew in love and in spirit is not dead, that only the body is gone, perhaps they would mourn less.
>
> I have heard always that one lives on and on and on in the lives of people one has touched and that this is immortality. I accept this, but it is not enough for me. If the energy of this physical universe is never lost but only changes form, why not the same for the psychic energy of "me"? It has always seemed inconceivable to me that all that is built into a person should disappear with the stopping of a heart. If our Creator

conserves energy in the physical world, He would surely do so in the spiritual world of "being" and "becoming." . . .

Perhaps the spirit, the "person" part of me, has always lived, has been passed on from expression to expression of me over the millennia. This is an awesome thought, to be sure, but no more so than the mystery of our complex selves existing in the here and now.

Death, I do not fear you, but neither do I want you. I love too much of this life, and I love too many people. . . . But with all of the love and beauty here, surely there will be even more "there." I trust you, Death. You are not my friend, but neither are you my enemy.

Perhaps Victor Hugo said it better. . . . "When I go down to the grave, I can say like many others, 'I have finished my day's work.' But I cannot say, 'I have finished my life.' My day's work will begin the next morning. The tomb is not a blind alley; it is a thoroughfare. It closes on the twilight; it opens on the dawn."[8]

Our peace is found in the challenge of intimacy, the call to generativity, the triumph of integrity, and the trust in death. This is hope . . . this is peace . . . this is happiness.

---

8. C. Gilbert Wrenn, "The Future of a Person—Me," *Personnel and Guidance Journal* 54 (September 1975):20.

Marie R. Hofer, Ph.D., is a psychologist and full-time psychotherapist at the House of Affirmation in Montara, California. She studied at the Arnold T. Janssen College in Holland, received her master's degree at the De La Salle Graduate School in the Philippines, and her doctorate at the California School of Professional Psychology in San Francisco. From 1969 to 1972 Doctor Hofer expanded and coordinated the counseling and guidance services at FuJen Catholic University in Taiwan. She has taught languages in Italy and California.

Happiness as an Outgrowth
of Becoming an Individual

Marie R. Hofer

I am interested in happiness as the creative process of accepting, affirming, and expressing who we truly are. It is a goal all humans strive for in one way or another. It is a call to discover our center, from which we can balance and direct all our forces. In this sense I see happiness as owning a center, as being in charge of our lives, as becoming self-actualized.

Happiness then, for me, is the exciting yet difficult task of becoming and being an individual. This dramatic journey is as varied as people are varied. Nevertheless, there are some definite stages—rites of passage, so to speak—that humans seem to need to go through in order to arrive at a mature level of psychic presence. It is these common experiences that I will highlight in this article.

A person's life cycle can be divided into two major psychodevelopmental phases: from birth to midlife, and from midlife to death. Individuation, the psychological process of becoming an individual distinct from any other, generally happens, if it happens at all, during the second part of life. In my estimation this phase holds the potential for genuine happiness. To provide a clearer picture of the issues involved, let us first look briefly at the earlier phase of psychic development.

During the period from birth to midlife, our energy is predominantly outer-directed. Physical and emotional survival

37

is primary. We seek and establish our place in family and society. Our gaze is upon authority. We "learn the ropes," acceptable versus unacceptable behaviors, the shoulds and shouldnots. Unfortunately, we also learn to hide certain feelings and needs for the sake of acceptance by significant others. It is a period of adaptation to established rules and values. In adapting to these established norms we become citizens, and, in a way, part of the herd. The thrust during this first period is toward achievement: schooling, degrees, diplomas. From dependency on our parents we move toward the independent choice of a career. We build up our own circle of friends, we choose a life partner or a religious community. To a great extent, happiness during this period equals achievement of external goals.

While introduction to society happens almost automatically, the search for our own individuality needs specific attention. A seed will not reach its full potential unless it is given a very specific environment. As with many a seed, numerous persons never blossom into full self-realization. The words of the Bible seem to apply here: "Many are called, but few are chosen," or as I prefer to put it: "All are called, but few choose."

In the second part of our life cycle we confront a new challenge. When all the possible external goals have been reached, we often begin to experience a certain restlessness. This restlessness seems to arise from the center deep within us, indicating a growing anxiety over the meaning and purpose of existence. Questions such as: "Who am I?" "Where am I going?" "What do I want out of life?" begin to rise into consciousness. These questions pose the challenge, the divine calling if you will, to become a human being, separate and distinct from any other.

The search is now directed inward. Ambivalence and fear often block the way. As one of my clients recently reflected upon her initial struggle: "I was so afraid that if I looked inside myself, I might not find anyone there." It is like entering unknown land without a road map. Few people, therefore, make a deliberate choice to begin the process of self-exploration. Frequently, a crisis forces us to take a closer look at ourselves. The loss of a job, the death of a significant person in our life, a disappointment or growing self-doubt are examples of precipitating crises. We find the situation hard to handle, our distress may become increasingly visible, and we are forced down into what feels like total failure and helplessness.

I painfully recall a precipitating event in my own life. Although I had some awareness that not all was well with me, I was so busy covering up my inner discomfort by clowning, that I needed to be hit right between my eyes. So, one day, after I had been outrageously witty and funny again, a friend said to me: "I don't find this funny at all; in fact, I find you very pathetic. You are just putting on a show to cover up what's going on inside of you." I was so shocked I felt like fighting her: "You are right," I said angrily, "but tell me what I need to do to get out of this mess."

At the beginning of individuation, then, there usually is a point at which the person acknowledges: "I cannot go on like this. I have tried everything: a career change, alcohol, divorce, even attempted suicide. Nothing seems to alleviate my inner pain and unhappiness." Shame and embarrassment about such personal failure make it difficult to seek outside help. However, this is the time when people need a significant other to represent and objectify outer reality, since the inner reality is falling to pieces. It is usually at this point that friends and superiors stress the need for professional help and recommend a therapist. Quite some time, however, may elapse before the distressed person actually takes that step.

Essentially, the inner search is a confrontation with the dark side of ourselves: weaknesses, strengths, and unacceptable emotions that we have learned to be ashamed of and, as a consequence, repressed. Yet it is this "dark stuff" within us that holds the key to enlightenment and happiness.

The accompanying illustration summarizes my view of the journey into the self. The themes are familiar: crisis, fall, death, resurrection, ascension, and union. I call the two major dynamics involved "endarkenment" and "enlightenment."

At the beginning of a person's self-search, the focus is still predominantly outer-directed. Cause and cure, blame and control for personal unhappiness are sought in the outside world. Denial and blame are used: "Yes, I am unhappy—but if my husband weren't so aggressive . . . if my superiors weren't so damn controlling . . . if the world weren't so rejecting of me . . . I would be fine." As a therapist, I will usually pose the question: "But what if your husband, or superior, or the world isn't going to change?" Gradually, the client realizes that there is no other choice except to take responsibility for what is happening. This painful realization then opens the door to the exploration of the inner dynamics. The person becomes aware of aspects that had been repressed since childhood—needs, hurts, feelings, wants, hopes, strengths. It is a meeting with the shadow part of self. Shame and feelings of nakedness are common experiences at this level of insight. Nothing seems to make sense anymore. The "dark night of the soul" or the experience of "psychic death" becomes a painful reality.

An example may help to illustrate the growth process at this stage. A person, let us call him John, complains that his mother is a smothering, controlling woman who does not allow him to grow up. John views himself as a helpless victim of his mother's attitude. In exploring his feelings about this situation, he gradually becomes aware that he feels very attached to his mother, that part of him loves her solicitousness and part of him hates it. He also painfully realizes that he hides behind his mother's control to avoid facing his own fear of growing up. He becomes aware that he is not a helpless victim and that, unconsciously, he uses his mother to cover up his own psychic reality. Having obtained such insight, John now has a choice

The Process of Individuation

Union of Opposites

Self Expression

Ordinary Life

Crisis

Identity

Blame

Risk

Endarkenment

Enlightenment

Insight

Un-doing

Death-Choice = Rebirth

either to continue in his old victim ways or to begin to take responsibility for his own life.

At this point of realization, clients will frequently ask: "How can I get rid of all that negative stuff inside myself?" But there is no need to get rid of it. The ongoing challenge is the sorting out of emotions, needs, and wants: to acknowledge, accept, and express energies in healthier ways. Transformation, not destruction, is the answer. If I discover, for example, that I keep a lot of anger bottled up inside myself, I need, first of all, to learn to accept anger as a permissible feeling. Depending on the degree of repression, this process in itself may take weeks, if not months or years. Gradually I may decide to vent anger in an appropriate manner. In so doing, I will become aware of other anger-provoking events in my life. As a consequence of this awareness, I may decide to do something about them. In other words, I am beginning to channel my angry energy into productive activity. To the extent that I allow my energies to flow in positive ways, enlightenment begins to take place.

The unlearning and undoing of habitual, self-defeating responses is a process that requires much courage, risk taking, perseverance, and practice. People often stay in therapy for several years to get a basic grasp of what it means to be themselves. Much support is needed to face the risks and consequences of making creative changes. It may mean letting go of longstanding relationships, for example, if others are unwilling to accept our growing independence. Although such separations may be painful, the rewards of growing freedom, peace, and joy become very visible in the individuating person. Genuine smiles appear on the face, life appears to have meaning again, and personhood begins to feel indestructible.

At this point people may ask, "Well, why was I unhappy before and happy now? Nothing has really changed. I am still the same." Essentially, that statement is true, for indeed nothing much has changed. However, something very dramatic has happened internally: the energy that used to go into *hiding* unacceptable parts of ourselves is now flowing into *being* ourselves. Weakness and strength, foolishness and wisdom, darkness and light are all accepted as important forces within one's self. A marriage has taken place between the opposing realities. As one of my clients summed up her process: "I looked within myself, I hated what I saw, I embraced what I hated, and now I love myself."

Various degrees of happiness may, of course, be experienced at any stage in the individuation process, for instance, in mini-death and -resurrection experiences. To use the previous example, when John finally acknowledges that his dependency is *his* rather than his mother's problem, he may experience a certain relief and joy.

To achieve a more lasting *state* of happiness, it is necessary to work through all the major self-defeating dynamics. When that goal is achieved the challenge that remains is ongoing refinement and integration. Of course, happiness is not a stagnant state of being. As night follows day and day follows night, so needs the psychic energy to flow. At certain times enlightenment will seem to predominate; at other times, endarkenment. Quite often we will find ourselves back in the shadow state; but everything will be processed much faster into union, now that we have established basic self-respect and a healthier center on which to fall back.

I would like to use a classic fairy tale to summarize the challenge of individuation. Many persons look at fairy tales as having meaning only for children. This may be true of the watered-down Walt Disney renditions. However, if we look at the original classic versions, these stories, along with myths, have much deeper meanings. They may be looked at as representing the processes and stages of human psychic development to various degrees. I have chosen the story of Cinderella because almost everyone is familiar with it and because it seems to represent individuation in its entirety.

My second illustration mirrors the previous one, the only difference being that psychic states have now been replaced by fairy-tale characters.

Cinderella, so the narration goes, lives happily with her loving parents. Then her mother dies and the heart-shaking drama begins. The wicked stepmother and her daughters come onto the scene. They take over immediately, establishing roles of superiority and inferiority, and playing their oppressive games to the hilt. Cinderella, seemingly a helpless victim of their powers, sinks into ever-greater servitude and martyrdom.

The nasty stepcreatures obviously represent Cinderella's shadow side: the hostility, superiority, beauty, and power that she does not want to acknowledge within herself are projected onto other characters. Thus, she is almost totally controlled by the denial of her own negativity. The victim position, as uncomfortable as it may be, is often much more acceptable and may even feel virtuous.

Are pain and aches all there is to life? First faintly, but then louder and louder this question begins to stir in Cinderella's mind, prompted by the message from the kingdom that there is a prince to be won, a ball to be attended. This inspiring news gives birth to some small but unknown strengths within her. She is encouraged to the point of *doing* something about her miserable lot. So, Cinderella, who has not dared to open her mouth for years, other than to say "yes, madam," ventures to faintly mention her desire to attend the regal affair. This unfamiliar behavior on the part of the Cinder Maid is met with much uproar. We know of the endless tests and shenanigans her stepmother puts her through as a result of this assertive move. Obviously, this increased hostility symbolizes Cinderella's old self-depreciating attitudes, which seem to become even stronger as she grows more self-aware. Cinderella begins to realize that she will have to do something very drastic to escape this suppressive, negative influence in her life. Repression begins to give way to insight. Out of this growing determination a new character comes onto the scene: the fairy godmother. As the symbol of healthy nurturance, she represents creative change. Moved by

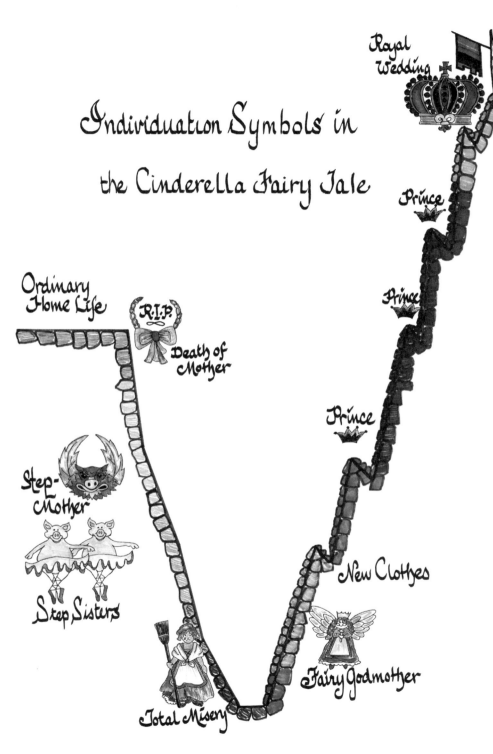

Individuation Symbols in the Cinderella Fairy Tale

Royal Wedding

Prince

Prince

Prince

Ordinary Home Life

R.I.P.

Death of Mother

Step-mother

Step Sisters

New Clothes

Fairy Godmother

Total Misery

this new energy and determination, Cinderella begins to make real what seemed impossible. She goes on a shopping spree, so to speak, defies her feelings of inferiority, and makes herself attractive enough to charm the prince. Three times, which means many, many times, she undertakes very ingenious but risky escapades. With each time her hope to conquer the prince's heart, and thereby to become free, grows by leaps and bounds. We know of the final hurdles: the stepdaughters' last, desperate attempt to deceive the prince and make their feet fit the mystery slipper—one of them by cutting off her big toe, the other one by cutting off her heel. But all the *good* forces are with Cinderella. The royal wedding takes place and, as the story goes, they live happily ever after.

Again, nothing really has changed. All the characters are still present, but now they are put in their proper places. Cinderella is still all of them, but she is no longer controlled by them. The prince obviously represents enlightenment, the opposite of the shady relatives. The marriage symbolizes the happy union of the opposites.

Some years ago, when I was traveling in Switzerland, I had an opportunity to converse briefly with Carl Jung's son. I was deeply moved by a thought he quoted from his father: "One of the saddest things Western thinking has done is to polarize divine powers into good and evil forces, that is, God and the devil." To me, God is the balanced union of darkness and light. We, who are made in his image and likeness, are called to serve him by becoming individuals and thereby achieving dynamic happiness.

Reverend J. William Huber, Ph.D., is assistant director and full-time psychotherapist at the House of Affirmation in Webster Groves, Missouri. A priest of the diocese of Pueblo, Colorado, Father Huber received his undergraduate education at St. Thomas Seminary in Denver. He completed graduate work in marriage counseling at the University of Detroit, and received his doctorate in clinical psychology from the California School of Professional Psychology in San Diego. Before joining the staff of the House of Affirmation, he was the founding director of the Pueblo Diocesan Office for Family Life. Father Huber also served in various other pastoral and associate pastor positions before undertaking his graduate studies. He is a member of the American Psychological Association, the American Association of Marriage and Family Therapists, and other professional organizations.

Addicted to Happiness: Now or Never

J. William Huber

Carefully guarded by thick glass and under the watchful eyes of security police, a document most precious to the United States is enshrined in our nation's capital. It is the Declaration of Independence. This document states that United States citizens have a right to life, liberty, and the pursuit of happiness.

More than two hundred years have passed since the signing of that great document, and we continue to possess the precious right to pursue happiness, although many other facts of our lives have changed. And what a pursuit ours has been.

Several states now list as their number one industry "tourism," a business that caters to the pursuit of happiness. Luring people from far and near, some states merchandise happiness in the form of Disneyworld, the Grand Canyon, Las Vegas casinos, and the Louisiana Superdome.

Happiness is also claimed as the product of the ever-growing electronics industry. One's wish to view ballgames and shows that are televised simultaneously is no longer a problem: videotape recorders can solve the dilemma. Because we are attracted to promises of instant happiness, we are told that we *can* have what we want when we want it!

In a land of instant coffee, instant replays, instant credit, and instant debt, we find it difficult to experience delays in our life. When we do meet delays, we tend to become instantly critical, forgetting that the Declaration of Independence promises only the *pursuit* of happiness; each of us must catch up with it by ourselves.

Our national obsession with happiness reminds me a bit of the man who was asked whether he ever worried about his dog, who had the habit of chasing every truck that went past his house. "Heck, no," said the old man, "I only worry about what the dog would do if he caught one." If one ever "reached" happiness, I wonder whether that person would know what to do.

Church and Happiness

In 1965 the Second Vatican Council ratified another important document, the Constitution on the Church. That constitution stated that "happiness" is a right of every person. It acknowledged that "human progress can serve man's true happiness" provided it is "purified and perfected by the power of Christ's cross and resurrection."[1]

In the 1963 "Decree on the Instruments of Social Communication," the Vatican II fathers also acknowledged that the moral order will lead humankind "to a rich measure of fulfillment and happiness."[2]

Thus the documents of the Second Vatican Council take note that the pursuit of happiness is natural to human beings and is a right of all people but that it can be reached only through moral means. Happiness is a good to be sought.

More recently, in 1976, the National Conference of Catholic Bishops stated that seminary life should produce "happiness" as well as holiness in the formation of the clergy.[3] They also encouraged novitiates to be places where each person in training for religious life feels fully appreciated and where the members contribute "to the happiness . . . of the community."[4]

---

1. *The Documents of Vatican II* (New York: The Guild Press, 1966), p. 235.
2. Ibid., p. 322.
3. *The Program of Priestly Formation* (Washington, D.C.: National Conference of Catholic Bishops Publication Office, 1976), p. 18.
4. Ibid., p. 129.

All this stress on happiness in our nation's Declaration of Independence, in the Constitution on the Church, and in the directives of our own hierarchy makes one wonder why the unhappy clergy and laity in today's Church are paying such a price. Every man and woman was created to be happy; this is the normal state of human affairs. To be "unhappy" is to be "abnormal" in some measure. It is too high a price to pay. Yet many go through life seeking happiness, not knowing what will bring it but feeling quite sure that what they have is not it.

Happiness Lost

If you are a vowed celibate, recall the day you dedicated yourself to the priesthood through ordination, or to your religious way of life through your vows. In the excitement of giving ourselves totally to God, most religious and priests expected to be filled with an inner peace following the turmoil of making their decision. Some of us anticipated a security we had not known before. With these hopes went the knowledge that we had "arrived" at last.

But all too soon, almost imperceptibly, the feelings of joy and fulfillment began to slip away. The painful question of vocation stared some men and women straight in the eye, and they began to wonder, "Is this all there is?" or "Is this what I really wanted?" Whatever they thought they must do to be happy seemed to bring more frustration than joy. The religious "honeymoon" was over.

In this stage, pessimism can abound.[5] We may believe that we have made a big mistake and thus become failures. Thoughts of leaving religious life may be frequent; withdrawing from our religious vocation may seem the only alternative.

If we do not carry the frustration to such an extreme, we may become cynical and begin to believe that there is no sense in trying to be happy. This cynicism may be expressed in statements

---

5. See Pierre Teilhard de Chardin, *On Happiness* (New York: Harper and Row, 1966), p. 15.

such as: "Why try to be a better priest? Nobody pays any attention to the priest anymore," or "No use trying to teach the little monsters in school. They really don't want to be there anyway." We may cynically believe that all most parents want is for the religious or priests to be the world's disciplinarians and "make" children behave when the parents themselves have not been able to do so.

Teilhard de Chardin noted that this attitude can be recognized when one says, "What is the good of trying to find the answer? . . . Why not leave the savages to their savagery and the ignorant to their ignorance? . . . And all this amounts to saying, at least by implication, that it is better to be less than to be more."[6]

Religious Pleasure Seekers

If we have been able to escape the pessimistic or the cynical approach to vocation, we may not so easily escape the pleasure-seeking approach. When all we do and attempt ends poorly, we can easily develop the attitude that happiness must be sought moment by moment, or it will elude us. Rather than giving up on life as the cynic and the pessimist are wont to do, the "pleasure seeker" believes that to live "does not mean to act, but simply to take your fill of this present moment."[7]

Clerical pleasure seekers may be the priests or religious who live for fancy clothes or for gourmet meals in the best restaurants, or who become connoisseurs of the best wines without regard to price. The pleasure seeker can also be the religious who cultivates people only to obtain a new community car, or to become the recipient of an all-expense-paid vacation, or to be invited to affairs of state the working person cannot afford to attend. Although there may be nothing immoral about any of these actions, the pleasure seeker does it all in the name of virtue, stating, "Look what I've given up. I have no spouse. I've renounced material ownership. Therefore, I have a right to enjoy such pleasures when I can obtain them. They are my due."

---

6. Ibid., pp. 16-17.
7. Ibid., p. 17.

It is interesting that the more successful persons become in collecting these skills and achieving positions of prestige, the more happiness appears to elude them. The harder people seek happiness, the less loving, the less peaceful, the less contented they find themselves. One would think just the opposite, that having these pleasures and these benefits would create a happy life, but what happens is that an internal mental addiction keeps such a person from enjoying life.

Sometimes pleasure seeking may be less obvious, as when a person really believes that a particular appointment or position will bring happiness. Yet the more the individual seeks the appointment or the position, the less happy he or she may be.

Religious Addiction

Let us call these people addicts, for this is what they are.[8] They are addicted, not to mood-altering drugs or alcohol, but to their own expectations. They are addicted to expected results—to finding happiness now or never. A man or woman can become addicted to any number of things: to a special friend, to a favorite restaurant, to a suite of rooms, to a particular appointment.

Addictions bring with them their own fears. They can cause jealousy if we are afraid another person may steal our source of fulfillment. For example, is the person you feel closest to paying more attention to someone else? Addictions can cause cynicism if they are not fulfilled, boredom if we seem to make little or no progress toward fulfilling our expectations. As any addict knows, addictions cause worry when we no longer can count on a steady supply of what we are addicted to. Addictions can cause

8. Some ideas from this section are taken from Ken Keyes, Jr., *Handbook to Higher Consciousness,* 5th ed. (Saint Mary, Ky.: Living Love Publications, 1975). Other ideas are the result of my experiences in working with persons addicted to substance abuse and sentenced by the Federal Bureau of Prisons to participate in the Narcotics Addiction Rehabilitation Act Program.

anxiety if we worry about being worried. But most of all, our addictions may cause unhappiness when the world fails to supply whatever we are addicted to.

People addicted to their expectations attempt to live by rearranging and changing the world of people and things outside themselves in order to obtain the object of their addiction. In this behavior, they resemble the drug addict who may steal, kill, or cheat to obtain the necessary drug. Yet, unlike the drug addict, they find it easier to hide an addiction to seeking happiness under the guise of having a right to it. Happiness is not an emotion, however, nor is it only pleasure. Pleasure is the fulfillment of a desire or an inclination, whereas happiness is a state of well-being and contentment. "Happiness without joy is unthinkable; but joy and happiness are two different things."[9] Thus, pleasure does not necessarily bring happiness. Neither does unhappiness come from conditions outside oneself, but from thoughts within. Unhappiness is the result of the patterns within one's mind.

Some of the addictive patterns that seduce one into believing happiness will follow if one's desire is satisfied may include the following or any variation thereon: "If only I can become pastor of that parish, I will be happy." "If only my superior would listen to me, I would be happy." "If only I can get out of this work, I will be happy." "If only I could become a member of that small community, I would be happy." "If only I could have my own private apartment, I would be happy." "If so and so were elected provincial, I would be happy." One may even tell oneself, "If only I could get a graduate degree, I'd be happy." But are the people with master's degrees or doctorates really any happier than those who lack them?

Some tell themselves that if only they could find the right person to love or to be intimate with, they would be happy. But their search for the right person does not end in happiness, especially if they have not yet learned how to love. Rather than learn this lesson, they may decide that they simply have not found the

9. Josef Pieper, *Happiness and Contemplation* (New York: Pantheon Books, 1958), p. 43.

correct person, and the vicious cycle is repeated again and again without success. Such people never seem to discover that *being* the right person is more important than *finding* the right person.

Addictive Backgrounds

Where does this addictive programming begin? Psychologists have long believed that it commences in the first few years of life. For example, most infants attempt to climb the furniture in their parents' home and, much to their mother's displeasure, secure a precious knickknack. The infant then experiences the object being taken forcefully from its grasp, and cries because it is being dominated and controlled by a more powerful person.

From such a seemingly insignificant incident, the infant begins ever so slowly to develop ways and programs to satisfy the developing addiction. Maybe the child will wait until mother is out of the room; (later as an adult, one may think: "If only I were in charge here, I'd be happy"). The infant may try to get an older sibling to turn over the desired object; (later one may believe: "You can make me happy"). After all, the denied object must be worthwhile, or why would mother take it away?

In similar ways, from very early in life, persons program themselves to feel that they must gain control or must manipulate others in order to be happy. Years later they may remain programmed to the addictions of earlier years—thinking that someone or something or some event will magically bring happiness—rather than learning that happiness is a process, a *quality* of life, not an object or person to be possessed.

Addictions are erroneous beliefs that trigger personal responses when the world does not fit into our desires. Frequently I encounter in my work as a psychologist well-intentioned persons who are addicted to "perfection." Perfectionists mistakenly link perfection with salvation. They have trouble differentiating major and minor imperfections, and "feel just as guilty after leaving the bed unmade for two hours," or their desks in disarray for a morning, "as they do ignoring a friendship for two months."[10]

Addictions to unrealistic goals may well be a hazard unique to the religious and priestly vocations. For example, rather than viewing perfection as a relative quality in process, many religious hold the unrealistic expectation that they can actually become "perfect" in this life. Some expect that therapy will "completely" or "perfectly" remove all blocks to their growth, and they will become "perfectly mature" and "perfectly happy" adults. When this process takes longer than expected, or when the results do not produce the perfection they expected, unhappiness and disappointment follow. Such "magical thinking circumscribes and constricts one's life."[11]

What we need to develop are preferences, or choices, rather than addictions. Choices leave us responsible and in charge of our own life.

Addictions or Preferences?

Addiction to results always causes unhappiness sooner or later. Preferences never do. When a preferred result is not accomplished or fulfilled, we avoid disappointment because it was only a choice, not a demand. Preferences will never make a person unhappy, no matter what the outcome; addictions lead only to unhappiness. Preferred goals may be attained; but results that are demanded can never be achieved because "enough" is never really enough. In addition, the nice thing about a preferred result is that when it is realized, we feel happy and grateful.

The only elements we can realistically afford to be addicted to are the *physical* necessities of life: air, shelter, and food in reasonable amounts. All other addictions to results are unhealthy and lead to unhappiness.

We distinguish between an addiction and a preference by paying attention; specifically, by paying attention to the signs of our

10. James W. Jolliff, M.D., *Too Much of a Good Thing* (Waco, Tex.: Self-Control Systems, 1980), p. 56.

11. Ibid., p. 49.

discomfort in various situations and noticing the expectations and desires we feel at that time. These emotions can be our best teacher and best friend.

If we reflect upon these feelings rather than react to them, the feelings will help us discover our addictions. If you are addicted to expecting your typewriter, your car, or your sewing machine always to be in working condition, you will suffer when it does not work. Beneath the feeling of unrest when your machine is out of order you will discover your demand to have peace at all times, or to be omnipotent, or never to feel angry. By contrast, if you *prefer* these machines to work well, you need not compound the problem by superimposing uncomfortable emotions on the reality of their disrepair.

It is far easier to believe that unhappiness is the result of somebody or something outside ourselves than it is to admit that the real source may be within. To admit that our internal expectations and thoughts may be the real culprit requires that we take responsibility. When someone else does anything that does not conform to our own addictions, it is the very addiction that creates the unhappiness, not the other person or action.

There is a story told of a pastor who was interviewing some prospective associates to be assigned to his parish. During the interview with the first applicant, the young priest asked what the parishioners were like. The pastor responded with a request: "Tell me how they are where you are stationed now."

"Terrible," came the reply. "The people where I am have no time for me. They criticize almost everything I do, they demand too much, and they ring the doorbell at the most inconvenient times. I just have to get out of there."

"Well, Father," the pastor replied, "they're the same here."

When the next applicant came a few days later, he too inquired about the parishioners. Again the pastor asked him what they were like in the parish where he was ministering.

"Just wonderful," the second priest replied. "They are going to the bishop to see if they can get me to stay. They cannot do enough for me. They have always been very considerate and most willing to cooperate, but I feel it is time to move on."

"Well, Father," the pastor again replied, "they're the same here."

If the pastor sounds a bit contradictory, stop and consider that a peaceful person lives in a peaceful world. An angry person creates an angry world. Unhappy persons can expect to meet others who respond in unhappy ways. But happy persons generally find their world populated with happy people. Each situation is a self-fulfilling prophecy. It is not what or who is outside ourselves but the enemy within that creates our unhappiness.

Pessimistic, addicted persons tend to be pessimistic because the world of their experience has not permanently fulfilled their expectations. This situation leaves them unhappy. Pleasure-seeking addicts are not very happy either. They live only for the present. When the present fails to deliver the object of their expectations, they can only be unhappy.

To live only in the past and relate solely on the basis of what has been leaves us feeling abandoned, afraid that life is passing us by. To live merely for the present moment is to fail to risk anything for the sake of the future. The fear of losing out makes us rather myopic.

Ongoing Discovery

Those who look toward the future will find life "an ascent and a discovery."[12] What an adventure that is! To "live" is to enjoy an unfolding discovery of reality without any preconceived expectations or demands about what will bring happiness. Such living encourages and brings about personal growth and development. This evolutionary process, according to Teilhard de Chardin, leads to true happiness, which is a "happiness of growth," an ongoing process. Furthermore, because the process is ongoing, happiness does not come to an end.

One way to examine how this happens is to observe ourselves whenever we enter into any situation, be it a therapeutic meeting, the sacrament of reconciliation, a medical examination, or just a visit home to our parents. If we do not enter into these

---

12. Teilhard de Chardin, *On Happiness,* p. 19.

situations with an open mind but rather go into them with pre-conceived hopes, fears, or expectations, our chances of coming away happy will be greatly reduced, if not totally demolished.

How often I hear of people who go home for a visit, expecting at last to be able to really "be at home" with one another and to rest, only to discover that their parents have planned a family outing to Aunt Tillie's. The hoped-for home visit turns into an unexpected and disappointing day elsewhere, and they return to the convent or the rectory unhappy and confused about their feelings.

As a therapist, I likewise have hopes and expectations for the people with whom I work. But if I enter into the therapeutic encounter demanding that certain things have to happen during that hour, I most certainly will end up defensive, communicating ineffectively, and angry when my demands are not met. So will the other person. Preconceived expectations stand in the way of meeting the real "other" and gaining happiness for both the "other" and for myself.

I likewise must help the client to acknowledge that I am human also. As a therapist, I have no magical qualities or secret source of knowledge that will make another person happy. Only through our relationship in therapy, through our hard work together in a supportive, nonpreconceived relationship will a person be free to explore alternatives and widen his or her outlook on life. But it is very disappointing for clients to realize that the therapist is human and cannot do the therapeutic work for them. The therapist can only help the individual explore personal patterns of thought and expectations; after examining the addictions together, the therapist helps the client withdraw from them.

Most people who enter therapy fear that they will be found "crazy." They also hope that they will spontaneously change without effort on their own part. This expectation is unrealistic: an addiction that can cause unhappiness in ever-increasing measure.

Paul Tillich once stated that happiness is possible even in pain and suffering. I agree with him. Everything rests on our own perspective. If we are willing to travel through life with fewer demands, we certainly will carry less weight on the journey! "In the achievement of happiness, it is essential to transform troubles into triumphs. One of the first steps is to gain a proper perspective of our difficulties."[13] We need objectivity; internal addictions cannot bring objectivity into our lives.

Much of what I have proposed herein goes against the American consumer mentality. The psychology of advertising is aimed at convincing people that happiness can be bought and sold. In the early 1980s we all know what happens when E. F. Hutton speaks!

All of us pursue happiness as our right, but for many of us, the pursuit becomes not a choice or a decision but an addiction.

Happiness is Decision

The pursuit of happiness always involves a decision. We participate in our own happiness as well as in our own unhappiness. Happiness and unhappiness are decisions we make.

It is like the little girl who told her mother that she had had a very happy day. "Really?" the mother asked. "What made today any happier than yesterday?"

"Yesterday my thoughts pushed me around," the little girl replied, "and today I pushed my thoughts around."[14]

The little girl was already learning the difference between addictions and choices or preferences. When our thoughts push us around, we are addicted. When we push our own thoughts around, we are in charge and can make our own choices.

To take charge of one's life, to become more fully responsible for oneself was the focus and hope of the Second Vatican Council fathers. They attempted to hand back personal responsibility

---

13. Kenneth Hildebrand, *Finding Real Happiness* (London: Purnell and Sons, 1957), pp. 164-65.

14. Ibid., p. 33.

for life choices to the individual Church members. However, instead of making some men and women happier, the responsibility returned to these individuals caused them tension and fear. In an age when people demand more happiness and freedom without responsibility, such accountability was bound to disturb those most addicted to irresponsible freedom.

Unhappiness may also have been created in persons who feared making mistakes because they had been addicted to childish dependency upon the authorities in their life. Furthermore, these individuals may have "idealized" what they understood to be "perfection" and seen themselves as failures.

It is not easy to accept responsibility when your past training rewarded you for being passive, for being submissive, and for maintaining silence. Difficult? Maybe. But definitely possible.

"Happy are the poor in spirit; theirs is the kingdom of heaven" (Matt. 5:3). The Lord invites us to divest ourselves of our addictions and to discover that happiness will be found only in our poverty of preconceived ideas and demands. Ours cannot be a "happiness, now or never!" mentality. Rather, life must be an ongoing process wherein happiness leads to heaven, too!

Reverend Thomas A. Kane, Ph.D., D.P.S., is a priest of the Roman Catholic Diocese of Worcester. His undergraduate studies were pursued at St. Edward's University, Austin, Texas; his graduate studies at National University of Mexico, Rutgers University, and St. Bonaventure University; and his postgraduate studies at Boston University and the University of Birmingham, England. As an educator and psychotherapist, Father Kane is a consultant to several Roman Catholic and Protestant groups. He is a frequent lecturer to academic and medical communities in the United States and Europe and a visiting scholar at Harvard University. He is a member of several professional organizations and serves on the board of directors of the National Guild of Catholic Psychiatrists. He is international executive director of the House of Affirmation and the author of several publications.

Happy Are You Who Affirm

Thomas A. Kane

Happiness is not in our circumstances, but in ourselves. It is not something we see, like a rainbow, or feel, like the heat of a fire. Happiness is something we are.
John B. Sheerin

When I was a little boy, I learned from my mom and dad that "God made me to know him, love him, serve him, and be *happy* with him in this life and in the next." It seemed that God and my parents wanted the same thing for me—happiness. Thus, I grew up thinking that happiness is what life is all about. In fact, upon entering adulthood, I learned that everything people do—their goals, aspirations, and dreams—revolves around happiness. Faith, love, religion, achievement, friendship, sex, recognition, vocation—everything that is important to us is a means to achieving happiness, and we do our best to change whatever interferes with that happiness.

As Americans, our Declaration of Independence states our right to "life, liberty, and the pursuit of happiness." The philosopher George Santayana wrote, "Happiness is the only sanction of life; where happiness fails, existence remains a mad, lamentable experiment." Saint Thomas Aquinas, whose teachings echo through the centuries, emphasized that "by nature, a person endowed with reason wishes to be happy and therefore cannot wish not to be happy!"

When was the last time you read anything about happiness? When was the last time you talked with somebody about happiness or heard a sermon, a lecture, or even participated in a good discussion about happiness? When was the last time you thought about happiness? Was it while watching a television quiz show offering prizes to make you happy, or the commercial that promised instant happiness if you used such and such toothpaste? Was the last time you considered happiness when you received the pay increase that would allow you to buy more things? Happiness posters abound these days. I saw one the other day which said, "Happiness is having a fuel-efficient car," and still another that said, "Happiness is having it twice daily." I do not know what "it" referred to, but I can imagine. A friend of mine wears a tee shirt that states, "Happiness is owning an English bulldog."

What is Happiness?

If we look at some American studies of attitudes we find that most Americans are really happy people. The results of a *Psychology Today* questionnaire indicated that sixty percent of the respondents had been "moderately happy" or "very happy" in the last six months. A survey published by the popular family magazine *Good Housekeeping* reported even more happiness— seventy percent of the respondents stated that they had been "moderately happy" or "very happy" over the last six months.[1] There are other more scientific studies, I am sure, but I think it is valid to state that most Americans are happy. This is true despite the obvious fact that this country has been experiencing difficult times in the form of inflation, unemployment, political corruption, and general upset in values.

It has been my privileged position to travel and lecture extensively in many parts of the world. I must honestly report that what I observe specifically true of Americans, I find generally true of most persons in our world, some of whom live in political

---

1. Jonathan Freedman, *Happy People* (New York: Harcourt, Brace, Jovanovich, 1978), p. 36.

turmoil and unspeakable living conditions; namely, most people are indeed happy.

What makes men and women happy varies considerably. The many elements that contribute to happiness can be divided into groups:

1. *The Social*—marriage, family, friends, children;
2. *The Economic*—job, income, standard of living, financial security;
3. *The Personal*—success, personal growth, physical and mental health, freedom, independence;
4. *The Spiritual*—leisure time for reflection, internal peace, faith, religion, belief in the absolute.

Happiness is Relationship

The complexity of human living certainly testifies that there is no simple recipe for producing happiness. However, poets, songwriters, philosophers, and theologians as well as the immediate authority of every living human being point to one necessary ingredient—some kind of intimate relationship. Relationship is what life is all about: relationship with one's world, self, others, and God.

Christianity is all about relationship. Its essential teaching is that when persons are respectfully intimate with their lover, friend, neighbor, God, and world, the result is happiness "in this life and the next." In fact, so important is relationship in Christian theology that it teaches that the love relationship of Father for Son and Son for Father results in a Person—Love—whom we call the Holy Spirit.

Affirmation is all about relationship. As we progress in this article we will consider affirmation and see how the *product* of affirmation is indeed happiness. Because there are many elements related to happiness, it is impossible to list a set of requirements that necessarily will bring about happiness. However, we do know that those who affirm and are affirmed are happy people. The affirmed person learns how to live life to the fullest, no matter what the life circumstances happen to be.

It is within the context of relationship and human sexuality that I wish to make this presentation. I choose to emphasize the role of relationship and human sexuality for the priest and religious in reference to happiness, because I think it is a vital and crucial question that must be open to discussion.

Relationship: Affirmation of Human Sexuality

Not long ago I saw a TV repeat of *All In The Family*. Archie Bunker lamented aloud to his wife Edith, "I don't know what the world is coming to with all those priests and nuns leaving, and breaking their vows of celebrity." Without intending to smother Archie's sense of humor in philosophical pathos, it could be observed that a vow of "celebrity" or "celebration" might indeed, if actually lived, attract many persons to the Roman Catholic Church and serve to inspire others to a life of love and fidelity in the priesthood and religious life.

It is important for me to state to my readers how I view myself, as I share with you in this article. I do so as a man who has chosen and chooses to be a Roman Catholic priest. With a mission given to me by my bishop, I see myself as a diocesan priest who uses psychology as an instrument of ministry. I do not see myself as a hyphenated priest, a priest-psychologist. I have been trying for many years to resist the priest-hyphen definition. My fundamental definition is as priest and not in terms of my avocation. To repeat, I share with you as a pastor of souls who employs the behavioral sciences as an instrument of ministry.

While you can certainly expect of me some scientific insight, I choose to share with you as a priest on pilgrimage with the issues of happiness, relationship, and human sexuality, and to offer you some reflections coming from the five House of Affirmation[2] therapeutic communities, four in this country and one in England, that I have helped to found. It has also been my privilege to have been invited to many dioceses and religious

---

2. Thomas A. Kane, "Psychotheological Therapy," *New Catholic Encyclopedia,* 1979, vol. 17, pp. 546-48.

congregations around the world in the last twelve years, and the reflections of this paper are influenced by my conversations with priests and religious and from my pastoral and clinical observations.

This presentation will center on the celibate's own sexuality, rather than a generalized discussion on human sexuality. Keeping this in mind, I will develop this paper in the following manner: first, some reflections on contemporary terminology concerning human sexual development; second, a consideration of human sexuality as an affirmation of relationship; and finally, some observations about preventive mental health in regard to priesthood and religious life.

Sexual Growth

In spite of the amount of literature available regarding sexuality, priests and religious as well as laity still lack sufficient knowledge of sexual growth and development. Although sexuality involves all the facets of the human personality—the physical, psychological, intellectual, spiritual and ethical—I wish to focus on the area of sexual growth. It is important to understand some of the contemporary terminology that has come out of recent sexuality studies.[3]

First, let us consider sex gender identity.[4] We know how important *in utero* is prenatal development of the fetus, and we are discovering every day genetic, hormonal, and fetal influences. However, when we speak about sex gender identity we are at the core of personality where the identity is being significantly formed. By two years of age, male and female know their gender identity. Little boys learn they are different from little girls and little girls know they are different from little boys. Phenomenologists refer to this stage of sexual growth as the biological

---

3. Frank A. Beach, ed., *Human Sexuality in Four Perspectives* (Baltimore: The Johns Hopkins University Press, 1976).

4. John Mooney and A. A. Ehrhardt, *Man and Woman, Boy and Girl: The Differentiation and Dimorphism of Gender Identity from Conception to Maturity* (Baltimore: The Johns Hopkins University Press, 1972).

phase. This physical identity of the child begins the sexual story of being a human male or female. Children discover that through the body they reveal themselves to others and to the world.

The following story illustrates the importance of sex gender identity. I was visiting my niece on a Sunday afternoon and brought my dog with me, a horrible creature, an English bulldog. As I sat talking with my niece the dog flopped down on the floor near her two and a half year old son. Suddenly we stopped our conversation as we noticed the boy and the dog. The child was rolling up the leg of his shorts and looking at his testicles. Then he looked at the dog, saw the dog had testicles, and said to me, "Uncle Tommy, the dog's got balls!" Needless to say, my niece was a little embarrassed at the slang that the youngster used. The important and very significant fact was the way my niece used the occasion to teach her little boy. "That's not the right word. Most males, and the dog is a male, have testicles." This experience of body and of discovering gender was quite different from that reported by a number of my clients during this period of curiosity. Many remember that their parents taught them the body is dirty, that the genitals are impure, and even now at forty or sixty years of age, they feel that gender is basically something very dirty, the body at best an occasion of sin.

Sex role identity in sexual growth appears to take on realized significance from age three and up. With sex role the child learns what society expects of a boy and girl, male and female. All cultures and societies teach and/or condition members as to the expected roles of male and female and have severe cultural penalties for nonconformists. Thus, little boys in American society learn to play with trucks and little girls learn to play with dolls. Obviously, there is much happening in society today that is changing role identity and making similarities less prejudicial. The result will be less sexism which is obviously healthy. However, it is important that we acknowledge the different role expectations and help the youngster to realize that the roles of male and female are not identical, physically or psychologically.

The phenomenologists refer to this aspect of sexuality as the cultural sphere of growth.[5]

Sex object preference is the third area of sexual development. Here the child is involved in sexual attraction; usually an individual can recall it from around the age of six. For most men and women the attraction is of a heterosexual orientation, that is, "sexual attraction to, or sexual activity with, members of the opposite sex."[6] About twelve percent of the population is of homosexual orientation, that is, "sexual attraction to, or sexual activity with, members of one's own sex."[7] Phenomenologists call the sex object preference the personal phase of development. New research indicates that a significant part of the population reports bisexual behavior in varying degrees.

Homosexuality

At this point, we can devote some attention to homosexuality, since it is a question of importance to the Church and society.[8] Note that the area of difference for the homosexual is not sex gender identity:, homosexual men know they are male, homosexual women know they are female. The difference surfaces in the area of sex role identity and sex object preference. We really do not know the precise origin of sex role identity or preference. However, there is a compelling amount of literature that points in the direction of learned or conditioned behavior during the early stages of postnatal and early childhood development.

Recently at a meeting on "Human Sexuality and Personhood" over two hundred Roman Catholic bishops heard a paper

---

5. Vincent M. Bilotta, "Sexual Emergence as an Access to the Spiritual Life," *Journal of Studies in Formative Spirituality* 2 (February 1981): 13-23.

6. James Leslie McCary, *Human Sexuality,* 2nd ed. (New York: Van Nostrand Reinhold, 1973), p. 343.

7. Ibid.

8. E. J. Franasiak, "Homosexuality and Related Myths of Unbelonging," *Belonging: Issues of Emotional Living in an Age of Stress for Clergy and Religious* (Whitinsville, Mass.: Affirmation Books, 1979).

by James A. Monteleone, Professor of Pediatrics and Adolescent Medicine at St. Louis University School of Medicine. Dr. Monteleone presented a brief synthesis of the physiological development of a person's sexuality. He offered the opinion that there is compelling evidence which suggests that the underlying influence on homosexual behavior is genetic. If homosexuality is scientifically proven to begin early in life, either *in utero* or shortly after birth, then the implications are enormous not only for the area of theology but also for the science of psychology as well.[9] However, the evidence regarding genetic predisposition at this time is incomplete and the data not very convincing. Genetics is an area of study still in its infancy regarding its eventual contribution to our understanding of human sexuality.

Regarding homosexual sex preference, Suzanne Breckel and Michael Murphy write:

> It is also clear that homosexual preference, notwithstanding traditional opinions to the contrary, does not necessarily imply any kind of social or behavioral degeneracy. Many homosexuals fall well within the normal range in such qualities as social competence, emotional stability, intelligence, efficiency and effectiveness in their work, and the ability to form naturally satisfying personal relationships, sexual and otherwise. Homosexual preference does not necessarily imply that a higher proportion of homosexuals than heterosexuals will encounter psychosocial difficulties. In many cases, this can be the direct result of the stress caused by social disapproval and fear of discovery. Whether homosexuality is a sickness or not will continue to be a subject for debate. However, for many it is a social disability because of stigma and minority status, and a personal disability because of the limitation of sex object choice. Thus, the homosexual life is neither glamorous nor particularly "gay."[10]

9. James A. Monteleone, "The Physiological Aspects of Sex," *Human Sexuality and Personhood,* published proceedings of the workshop of the hierarchies of the United States and Canada (St. Louis, Mo.: Pope John XXIII Medical Moral Research and Education Center, 1981).

10. Susanne Breckel and N. Michael Murphy, "Psychosexual Development," *Chicago Studies* (Spring 1981), p. 47.

Heterosocial and Homosocial Behaviors

At the same meeting of Roman Catholic bishops, Michael Peterson, a priest of the archdiocese of Washington and a psychiatrist, offered the following observations regarding the contemporary terms of hetero*social* and homo*social* behaviors.

In clinical practice one sees many patients who have adequate sexual arousal patterns as well as the necessary behavioral repertoire to engage in the genital aspects of sex. However, these patients may be unable to engage in the type of social behavior necessary for meeting, dating, and relating to persons of the opposite sex or the same sex.[11]

Fr. Peterson goes on to state that the social behaviors are very complex and are listed by different authors in various ways. He cites Tollison and Adams as dividing the components of hetero-social behavior into three elements: social behaviors necessary to initiate relationships with the opposite sex, social and inter-personal behaviors preceding sexual behavior, and behaviors required to maintain heterosocial relationships.

For example, the young person who is beginning to learn from role models and peers the methods of approaching the opposite sex must master four important skills:

1. Ability to ask open-ended questions;
2. Art of the extended conversation;
3. Conversation serving as an avenue for self-disclosure; and
4. Initiating relationships and appropriate eye contact.

Fr. Peterson maintains that similar types of social skills would be required for homosexually-oriented persons as they begin a lifestyle of initiating contacts and relationships with members of the same sex. The culture, however, would dictate different sur-roundings and different kinds of approaches depending on the setting such as a bar, a party, work, or a casual meeting.

It is clearest to researchers that these kinds of heterosocial and homosocial behaviors related to sexuality are learned and are

---

11. Michael R. Peterson, "Psychological Aspects of Human Sexual Behaviors," *Human Sexuality and Personhood*, p. 95.

related to certain proscribed and prescribed cultural norms and values.

Celibacy

The human sexuality of a priest or religious certainly does not exist in a vacuum. Interaction with the personalities of other men and women is needed just as sound does not exist unless it is perceived. The fall of a large tree in a forest is translated into sound only when the stimuli of the impact produce an effect on the auditory apparatus of a person or animal. In the same way, affirmation in the social sense does not exist unless the individual is involved in social relationships with others. This process implies constant communication. Normal human life cannot exist without human interaction. For priests and religious to understand their sexuality, they must interact with persons of their own sex and in significant degrees with those of the opposite sex. We approach every situation first as human beings who are male or female.

There is no doubt that marriage has a profound effect on a person's emotional life. So does the celibate life. The significance of the renunciation of genital sexuality has special meaning for the development of the emotional life. Rollo May says that "for human beings, the more powerful need is not for sex per se, but for relationship, intimacy, acceptance, and affirmation."[12] Erik Erikson notes: "Every truly mature man and woman must be capable of experiencing genital sexuality with a mature partner of the opposite sex. However, the same is true for its renunciation."[13] The behavioral sciences and important psychological studies point out that the need is not so much for genitality as for relationships that are either fully masculine or feminine.

---

12. Rollo May, *Love and Will* (New York: W. W. Norton, 1969).

13. Erik H. Erikson, *Insight and Responsibility* (New York: W. W. Norton, 1964).

For centuries the call to priesthood and religious life in the Western Church has invited and required human beings to transcend and sublimate genital sexual needs. Although priests and religious do have unconscious motivations, their conscious vocational goal is the fulfillment of a spiritual need based on Christian values. Today priests and religious are encouraged to develop human relationships as a sign of their deep and mysterious relationship with Christ. Celibacy as a way of life is meaningful only if it is a way of loving. It says something about a person's relationship to God only to the degree that it says something significant about human relationships—person to person. We priests and religious relate as body persons to other body persons. We are called to integral emotional relationships because the Christ by whom we are called is human, a man, as well as divine, God. God calls us because of our humanity and not in spite of it. The vitality of celibate witness can couple the negation of genitality with affirmation of other human beings and open us to receive their affirmation.[14]

Eschatological witness means little if the celibate's life is not a meaningful affirmation of his or her sexuality in the world. Jesus did not purchase his purity by removing himself from men and women but rather by being involved with them. Further, the resurrection affirms for humanity the active presence of Christ as a man, fully man, with manhood purchased not by simple negation but by affirmation of his humanity—an affirmation repeated in word and deed over and over again in the Gospel accounts.[15]

Discussing the role of human sexuality, Karol Wojtyla, now John Paul II, wrote:

> It is exactly in this that the fundamental ethical trait of love is expressed: it is an affirmation of a person—without this affirmation, love does not exist. Permeated with a proper attitude concerning the value of a person—and such an attitude we

14. I have expanded on this topic in my book *Happy Are You Who Affirm* (Whitinsville, Mass.: Affirmation Books, 1980).
15. John P. Dondero and Thomas D. Friary, *New Pressures, New Responses in Religious Life* (New York: Alba House, 1979).

termed affirmation—love reaches its fullness; it becomes what it ought to be: an integral love. Without this affirmation of the value of a person, love disintegrates and, in fact, does not exist at all, even if the reactions or experiences coming into play are of a "loving" (erotic) character.[16]

Healthy relationship then is the key for celibates in a lifestyle that is a compelling way to live out their sexuality. So important is this idea of relationship that the U.S. Bishops Committee on Priestly Life states:

> Too often, stress which has been placed on avoiding relationships effects a defensive style when priests relate with women, or when sisters relate with men, either socially or in ministry. Such style is particularly inappropriate today when men and women are expected to interact on a regular basis as co-workers as well as in social situations.
>
> Men and women must be able to interact in relationships which are mature, honest, responsible and appreciative. Such relationships presume a realistic degree of self-knowledge. Furthermore, they allow each person to realize his or her God-given dignity in the blend of femininity and masculinity within every person. This blend is God's gift to us and to each other. Men and women who are church ministers, as much as any other human persons, need one another's support in personal development. Celibate commitment must be a path toward the sort of independence, self-reliance and wholeness which make one capable of conscious self-sacrificing and loving relationships with others. Otherwise, it cannot be an appropriate lifestyle.[17]

Reductionism

This statement of the Bishops Committee could be very dangerous. What they stress as the way to maintain celibacy appropriately is not the way most priests and religious were trained. Many were educated in a manner that did not integrate their

---

16. Andrew N. Woznicki, *Karol Wojtyla's Existential Personalism* (New Britain, Conn.: Mariel Publications, 1980), p. 38.
17. U.S. Bishops Committee on Priestly Life and Ministry, *As One Who Serves* (Washington, D.C.: U.S.C.C., 1977), p. 65.

studies in scholastic philosophy with the intellectual and emotional life. They were exposed to a system that encouraged not a healthy discipline but fear of the emotional life. Freud was condemned in seminaries and by some schools of thought as a reductionist, for supposedly claiming that all human relations are sexual, that is, they end in bed. With regard to human relationships, seminarians and novices were taught to be on their guard not only with the opposite sex, but even with members of the same sex. What celibates heard explicitly condemned about Freud, they were implicitly taught about relations: all relationships will end in bed! Professors condemned the so-called reductionism of Freud but were often reductionists themselves regarding human relationships. The reality is that people go to bed with others because they choose to do so. Priests and religious who are now being encouraged in relationships, who are now being told this is where the celibate witness is most real, are often confused and suspicious because of their previous training. They enter relationships in a reductionistic manner, consciously or unconsciously thinking that indeed all behavior does become genital at some time.

Period of Awkwardness

If we are now encouraging celibates to enter into relationships as suggested by the fathers of Vatican II and the American bishops, then we must not be frightened by some of the awkwardness we see in growing relationships. We need to be open to new models of relationships between men and women. For example, vacations for priests with fellow priests are usually acceptable, and this is good; they are acceptable, if the vacation is with the priest's family, and this is frequently good; or, even with a group of five or six parish altar boys, and why this is good is often a mystery to me; but, what would we say to the priest who chose to go on vacation with a woman friend? I am not necessarily advocating this idea. I *am* saying that if we invite new insights and give new importance to male-female relationships, then we must be prepared for new models, new structures for relationships. Inviting mature male-female relationships will not only bring about a healthier understanding of celibacy but will also lead us to reflect on its options. This present period of what I choose to call *awkward growth* brings priests and religious to the point of asking difficult questions about their human sexuality. It is a time calling for a deep understanding of personal integrity and community responsibility. Celibates involved in relationships might ask and reflect on these questions:[18]

1. Am I growing in self-knowledge? Do I have a spiritual director or other Christian person who will ask me honest questions in my decision-making process?

2. Am I selective in my relationships? Or do I turn to the most needy or unhappy person for significant involvement?

3. Do I discuss the nature and meaning of mutual growth in the relationship in a reflective rather than reactive manner?

4. Do I open my life to relationships that are consistent with my lifestyle and celibate ideals?

5. Am I gentle with myself and others when speaking about the limits of relationship?

6. Does my relationship with another human being bring me to a position of new insight and appreciation of interior prayer and spiritual realities? Do I see myself and others as pilgrims on the different roads of adult Christian living?

I honestly believe that our priests and religious who are trying to live a life of relationships with others, sometimes very awkwardly, are at least in the race. What race? The race toward intimacy, intimacy with others and with God.[19] Priests and religious who are not in the race are easily recognized by their cold hearts, their boredom, their isolation marked by rugged individualism, their lack of the radiant warmth of Christ.

Viktor Frankl in his thought-provoking book, *The Unheard Cry for Meaning,* states that although the need for intimacy can

18. Anna Polcino, "Belonging—Longing To Be," *Belonging: Issues of Emotional Living in an Age of Stress for Clergy and Religious* (Whitinsville, Mass.: Affirmation Books, 1979), p. 102.

19. Thomas J. Tyrrell, *Urgent Longings: Reflections on the Experience of Infatuation, Human Intimacy, and Contemplative Love* (Whitinsville, Mass.: Affirmation Books, 1980).

drive a person to sexual promiscuity, it can also offer that person "an opportunity to meditate."

> People cry for intimacy. And this cry for intimacy is so urgent that intimacy is sought at any expense, on any level, ironically even on an impersonal level, namely, on the level of merely sensual intimacy. The cry for intimacy then is converted into the invitation "please touch." And from sensual intimacy it is only one step to sexual promiscuity.
>
> What is needed much more than sexual intimacy is existential privacy. What is greatly needed is to make the best of being lonely, to have the "courage to be" alone. There is also creative loneliness which makes it possible to turn something negative—the absence of people—into something positive—an opportunity to meditate. By using this opportunity one may make up for the industrial society's all too heavy emphasis on the "vita activa," and periodically spend some time on the "vita contemplativa." From this we may see that the real opposite to activity is not passivity but rather receptivity.[20]

Observations

In growing toward becoming responsibly closer to our neighbor, I suggest that priests and religious keep in mind the following observations about preventive mental health.

1. *Slow down, pause, stay still, and just BE.* Relax physically and mentally. To be a sign to the world, the priest or religious must have something of that counterculture that was Jesus' challenge to his world. This fact has implications in the areas of justice, functionalism, and the use of power. Many persons in ministry are so busy working in the name of the Good Shepherd that if he were to walk into the room they would be too busy doing "holy work" to see or recognize him. Yet priests and religious bear witness to Jesus, and must give priority to time for community and individual prayer and meditation.

2. *Be who you are.* Like Zacchaeus, priests and religious should work toward living with a self-image that is based on

---

20. Viktor Frankl, *The Unheard Cry for Meaning* (New York: Simon and Schuster, 1978), pp. 71-73.

reality and not on false idealism. They need to be reminded that they must sometimes say no and set limits on the demands that others make on their time and energy. A fine balance must be struck between helping others and being good to oneself. Religious and priests need to find outlets for creative recreation and hobbies, and to develop the ability to have fun and "waste time" enjoyably in ways that are enriching.

3. *Do not try to do everything.* Some priests and religious expect too much from themselves and are in a constant state of worry and anxiety because they are not achieving as much as they think they should. They try for perfection in everything. Admirable as this ideal is, it is an open invitation to failure. No one can be perfect in everything. Decide which things you do well and then put your major effort into these activities. They are probably things you like to do, that give you the most satisfaction. As for the tasks you cannot do so well, give them your best effort, but do not punish yourself if you cannot achieve the impossible. Congratulate yourself for the things you do well, but do not set yourself records to break in everything you do.

4. *Look for the goodness in others.* There is a tendency to consume too much valuable energy with introspective community reorganization and constant revamping of structures. This inward-looking tendency stifles the apostolic spirit of reaching out to others in their need. Meeting after meeting can have a very depressing effect on people. Instead, allow leisure time for the development of friendships with men and women of your own choice. Relationships in all their aspects are at the center of many problems in diocesan ministry and religious congregations today. Healthy appreciation of relationships with Christ and neighbor assures the continuity and fruitfulness of priesthood and religious life.

For healthy living, you should also set aside time for contemplative reflection on your own emotional and spiritual life in order to fully enjoy being alive and feeling.

5. *Enjoy your emotions.* All emotions are good. However, they may be comfortable or uncomfortable. God gave us emotions to teach us something about ourselves. We need to develop a healthy integration of intellect and will in order to desire and take delight in spiritual realities. A strong strain of moralism and idealistic perfectionism still compounds depressive guilt feelings and compulsive self-destructive behavior. Many of the neuroses I treat are aggravated by styles of spirituality and community life that encourage religious to be slavishly dependent, to intellectualize and mask the so-called negative feelings, and to try to be happy without giving and receiving genuine affection and warm love.

6. *Share conversation with friends.* A goal for each member of a diocese or religious community should be to discover and encourage every life-giving and affirming aspect of the total life situation of others. Priests and religious should see themselves both as healers and as needing to be healed by others.

We need honest and frank conversation without censuring or judging. There must be freedom to confront and challenge lovingly, in order to prevent an irresponsible permissiveness.

The local diocese or religious congregation becomes affirming when the members feel that they are free to be themselves, to make mistakes, and to find gentle forgiveness and deeply caring support. Our Church professes and proclaims that its root and cornerstone is incarnate love. Yet ironically, many priests and religious suffer because there is a devastating lack of love in their lives.

7. *Be assertive, not aggressive.* If we are aggressive, we tend to attack people or ideas. When we are assertive, we speak up for our own rights without infringing on the rights of others, and, in the process, improve our own self-image. I assert my ideas or feelings directly and honestly while allowing the other person to do the same. Assertiveness can teach us to look at ourselves and our behavior honestly and to express our wants openly without hidden or passive-aggressive agenda.

The "assertion" that pop psychology stresses is many times nothing more than old-fashioned selfishness or rudeness. Militant in tone and aggressive in manner, it is often merely an effective tool with which to put people down. Selfish and rude persons want things their own way and will allow little negotiation, compromise, or tolerance. Aggressive behavior puts people at a distance and fosters isolation. Continued nonassertion leaves the individual depressed and feeling like everyone's doormat. Growth in affirmation means growing out of nonassertive or aggressive behavior into an assertive posture. I often tell my clients that the affirmed person will have enemies. Not that we want enemies, but if we stand firm and do not allow others to violate us, we run the risk of being disliked.

Christian concern for one's neighbor is not obsolete. I am talking about a respectful approach to persons, a way of integrity and prudence that comes from a true understanding of humility. God commands us to love our neighbor as ourselves. If we and others have been created in the image of God as Genesis insists, we have no right to despise God's handiwork. Too often nonassertive behavior has been identified with humility, and assertion has been confused with the sin of pride. In this connection, it is refreshing to recall that Saint Thomas Aquinas's definition of humility is "the reasonable pursuit of one's own excellence." We could hardly find a more psychologically healthy statement. We have a God-given excellence and we are called to develop it in accordance with reason. Pride, then, would be the unreasonable pursuit of our own excellence. Nonassertive behavior in regard to our own personal integrity and aggressive behavior toward others do violence to God's plan. Learning to assert ourselves effectively and meaningfully is a path to affirming others and to opening ourselves to the affirmation of others.

8. *Realize that adult living is difficult work.* The celibate life is for adults only. During the last few years numerous how-to books have been offered to the reading public: how to be happy, successful, popular—*instantly*. This is nonsense. There is no

magic formula to make life easy. There is no quick cure for the problems we face in life and the weaknesses we find within ourselves. If we think that ministry should and can be always serene and easy, we are entertaining a naive childish fantasy.

There is a lot of sloppy miracle talk current today. Anyone who promises either a quick miracle or a fast cure is theologically and clinically irresponsible. Miracles do happen, miracles of grace, but to promise them as a common occurrence is to promise something that cannot be guaranteed.

Mature priests and religious realize that adult living is difficult work, that there is pain, tension, and anxiety in our days as well as happiness and peace. Because theology today emphasizes the Resurrection, we must not forget that Christ suffered the Gethsemane experience and travelled the Way of the Cross.

9. *Be gentle with yourself. Laugh a little.* Life is filled with incongruities. Everything does not depend on your efforts or mine. Jesus speaks to us when he says, "Learn from me, for I am gentle and humble of heart. Your souls will find rest" (Matt. 11:29). When we struggle to live the life of affirmation, we come to know and feel something of this intimate gentleness of Jesus as we see it reflected in our world, our neighbors, and ourselves.

In his book *Spirituality and the Gentle Life,* Fr. Adrian Van Kaam gives us an original and comprehensive study of gentleness as the facilitating condition and fruit of the Holy Spirit.[21] Van Kaam explains that gentleness does not point to a thing but to a person's attitude. Gentleness is usually sparked by something that is precious but vulnerable. A baby, little children, the victim of a tragedy, a holy person, a newborn puppy, a sick person, or the elderly can evoke gentleness. Strength and power do not elicit gentleness so much as do the fragility and the vulnerability of life. All that is delicate, innocent, and unblemished can, consequently, invite our gentleness. We experience it in our gentle response to a young child not yet tarnished by the harsh ways of the world.

---

21. Adrian Van Kaam, *Spirituality and the Gentle Life* (New Jersey: Dimension Books, 1974).

We feel gentle in the presence of a beautiful rose, the loneliness of a human face, and the dignity of gracious music. Any person, place, thing, or situation that mirrors the fragility of life brings forth the gentle person within us. All that is beautiful can make us gentle for it can be marred so easily.

10. *Pray.* Prayer is time spent with the Lord, fostering an affective relationship with him. In an atmosphere of loving trust, I can bring my other affective relationships to the Lord, so that they can develop under the guidance of his spirit without fear of reprisal or condemnation, since they also are God-given. Pray the prayer for affirmation:

> Jesus, inspired by the example of St. Therese, I place all my trust in your Sacred Heart, and surrender myself to your will. Come into my life, drive away my fears, stop my restless strivings, and show me new ways of pleasing you. Teach me to discern the good in others and to love them with an affectionate smile, a gentle touch, a patient ear, and an affirming word.
>
> St. Therese, pray that I will become alive again with awe and appreciation of Truth and the courage to oppose evil. Remind me always that I am created for happiness, for the joy of living in the presence of God. St. Therese, pray that I and all the friends of the House of Affirmation may have the inner peace that comes from confidence, surrender, and affirmation. Amen.

Conclusion

Early in this presentation I quoted Archie Bunker, and in doing so suggested that we consider priests and religious and human sexuality with the thought of celebration in mind.[22] To the extent that we celibates celebrate the reality of our sexuality—free men and women who choose to love our brothers and sisters in Christ in a personal and responsible manner—to that extent we are credible witnesses to the suffering of the Way of the Cross and to the happiness of the beatitudes.

22. Geoffrey B. Kelly, "Eunuchhood or Brotherhood? Another Look at Gospel Challenge," *Sexuality and Brotherhood,* (Lockport, Ill.: N.A.R.B., 1977).

The happiness that is produced by relationship is no quickly delivered accomplishment. It is produced by way of pilgrimage, a life journey that involves birth, pain, growth, change, and peace. Let us go to the mountain of the beatitudes. There we look at the Lord, listen to his word, and absorb his "happy are you." Through the Good News that he speaks to us we can understand what the Lord expects of us here and now. He is our affirmer. He is the way, the truth, and the life.

Let us forget for a while all our daily cares so we can listen intently to the message of the Lord. Soon we will realize that there is room for the images of our daily lives in the clear air on the mountain of the beatitudes. The Lord takes us infinitely seriously *just as we are.* He has a message for us that sheds light on our questions about life and happiness: "You are the light of the world" (Matt. 5:14).

The Beatitudes

How happy are the poor in spirit:
    theirs is the kingdom of heaven.
Happy the gentle:
    they shall have the earth for their heritage.
Happy those who mourn:
    they shall be comforted.
Happy those who hunger and thirst for what is right:
    they shall be satisfied.
Happy the merciful:
    they shall have mercy shown them.
Happy the pure in heart:
    they shall see God.
Happy the peacemakers:
    they shall be called children of God.
Happy those who are persecuted in the cause of right:
    theirs is the kingdom of heaven.

(Matt. 5:3-12)

Vincent M. Bilotta III, Ph.D., is a full-time psychotherapist at the House of Affirmation in Whitinsville, Masachusetts, and is chairperson of the department of formation ministry at the House. He did his undergraduate work in philosophy and psychology at the College of the Holy Cross, Worcester, and received his master's and doctoral degrees in clinical psychology from Duquesne University. He interned at USAF Wilfred Hall Medical Center in San Antonio, Texas, and served as a staff member at Scott AFB Medical Center in Belleville, Illinois. Here his interests included working in the area of death and dying, training family practice physicians and residents in psychiatry, and dealing with individuals, families, and groups in psychotherapy. In 1976 Dr. Bilotta joined the staff of the House of Affirmation. He is a member of the editorial board of *Studies in Formative Spirituality,* and lectures on formation topics to clergy and religious.

Happiness: A Path of Letting Go and Surrendering

Vincent M. Bilotta III

"I don't believe in happiness." This quote is not from the hard, miserly old Scrooge in Charles Dickens's *Christmas Carol*. It is not from the storyteller of the *Book of Job*. Neither is it a statement from one of my angry, depressed psychotherapy clients. I must admit that this quote is mine. It was my spontaneous "gut" reaction when I heard that happiness was the topic of our 1981 symposium.

When I volunteered to research this topic, I knew I would be signing up for both an adventure into the world of thought, scholarship, and reflection, and a personal search into understanding why I did not believe in happiness. The feeling that accompanied my statement was not sharp or intense. I simply felt "matter-of-fact" about it. But where did it come from? From what level of my consciousness did it spring? What did it mean? What story was this feeling statement telling about me? In a leisurely and playful manner, I listened to my experience of my statement "I don't believe in happiness" and contemplated it within the framework of my life story. In so doing, I was able to get in touch with the source of this reaction.

Personal Struggle

I was the oldest of eleven children. All thirteen people in my family lived in a five-room house, with six boys in one room and

85

five girls in another. Private space was practically nonexistent, and there was constant noise around the house. The pressures and tensions of "making ends meet" were always part of every-day awareness. My father worked very hard to provide for his family.

The perspective that "the world is a jungle" seemed to echo in my childhood experience. It was stressed that if you were going to survive, you had better know how to take care of yourself. Survival training was difficult work. I gradually internalized the strict and at times rigid discipline. There is no bending in the jungle; only the strongest survive. This survival-of-the-fittest mentality was reinforced throughout my formative years as the culture invited me to work hard, achieve, and become successful in whatever I did.

Throughout my life I continued to feel very supported and loved by my parents. They did the best they could, but it was still difficult for me to grow up and meet life's challenges. I learned survival training very well. I am grateful to my parents and the other significant people in my life. The strength that I acquired from that relatively secure space called home has assisted me in learning to adapt, survive, and be self-sufficient.

Idealism, Disappointment, and Cynicism

My childhood experiences encouraged idealism. Ideals were given to me to achieve, and, again, hard work was presented as the way to accomplish this task. Because it was clear that living should be a striving for perfection, I labored constantly to achieve the ideal.

The idealistic person pushes to realize ideals. Eventually, along the way, idealistic people become frustrated by the world's lack of response to their ideals, and disappointment begins to characterize their lives. Cynicism may be one response to this disappointment. There is also a gradual disbelief in the goodness and sincerity of others. No matter how hard one works to achieve ideals, people do not seem to be interested. A belief develops that people are motivated by their own selfishness.

As an idealistic person, I bring residual disappointment and cynicism from my childhood to each situation. At times, these experiences can color my perception of a situation. Thus, upon further reflection, I realized that my spontaneous reaction of "I don't believe in happiness" is part of that childhood residue of disappointment and cynicism.

Social and Professional Observations

Reading the daily newspaper does not encourage me to feel happy. The idealistic within me wells up and is saddened and angered by the violence, the greed, the stubbornness, and the pride in the world around me. How is it possible for me to be happy in the insensitive, superficial, uncaring world in which I find myself every morning when the media present the news of the day to me?

If I am awake, alive, and not hardened of heart, the reports on adolescents killing people for fun, the starving people in the Third World, the abandonment of our elderly, and the exploitation of the land, all pose the same question to me: "How can I be alive and open to this part of the human condition and still be happy?"

The tragedy of the divorce rate and its resultant numb, shell-shocked children makes it extremely difficult for me to imagine people being happy. Then there is the experience of sitting in my office listening to one tragic story after another. From my experience as a psychotherapist, I have come to use an image of what it was like for many people growing up from infancy to adulthood in this country. It appears to me that on a feeling level, these children were issued corsets that were tightened as much as possible around the abdomen. The corsets were so tight that it was even difficult to breathe. Children were also given a band that went around the chest like a bra. This band was also tightened to the point that it became difficult to breathe. Then the children were issued choke collars. The image of children with tight corsets, bras, and choke collars is indeed horrible. The obvious messages were "don't express your feelings" and "you must hold your feelings in at all cost." These images do not foster a sense of happiness within me.

So, struggling to understand my "gut" reaction to the theme of this year's symposium, I have discovered and claimed issues that emerge from my own childhood residue. These themes are: life is a jungle; it is the strong and well disciplined who survive and get ahead; life is hard work; and idealism, cynicism, and disappointment. Added to these themes are some social observations of everyday tragedy, and my personal observations of the way many children are taught to deal with their feelings. All these experiences seem to be part of my spontaneous statement: "I don't believe in happiness."

Second Reaction

My second "gut" reaction to the theme of happiness was that it had something to do with the process of becoming a peace-filled person. Inner peace emerges as people accept themselves, others, and human conditions as they are. We are all broken people with childhood residues of insecurity, vulnerability, and fragility. The deep peace that we are all seeking may flow from a "letting go" of our childhood residue of pride, and a surrendering to a path of humility.

This second spontaneous reaction to the theme of happiness originates also out of my own personal struggle to make sense of how to live my life. Through my own psychotherapy, I have made peace with residual issues from my childhood. Becoming aware of my personal pride was very painful; owning how fragile and vulnerable I am was a process of gradually accepting and surrendering to who I am in light of all that is. From this transformed perspective, the world was no longer a jungle to be dealt with, but rather a complex interrelationship of myself and others, interacting within the historical human condition. Struggling within this interrelationship, I find myself called to live with gentleness, compassion, respect, and reverence toward myself, others, and the world.

The survival training of hard work in which I was initially formed and that I had experienced as a burden to be carried, has been transformed into a creative gift. The path of letting go and of surrendering is hard work, requiring discipline, reflection, and decision. In the past I used to deal with my insecurities by fostering skills of mastery, control, and hard work, so as to survive and achieve a sense of security. I now find that I can take these personal, functional skills, which are good and helpful, and use them in the service of my more integrated growth process.

Happiness in Everyday Life

In order to examine happiness as it is lived out in everyday life, I asked people from the first grade through adulthood to describe in writing an experience of happiness in their everyday life. About nine hundred of them responded.

People reported that during such experiences, they felt in contact with their bodies. Their bodies felt so light, free, and easy that, at times, they actually felt they could fly. Breathing seemed easier, deeper, and slower. Body movement was spontaneous, graceful, harmonious, and coordinated, and they felt free from chronic muscle tension. Some were moved to dance, run, or sing. People also reported that their faces seemed alive and attractive: their eyes looked bright and sparkling, and their skin was soft, warm, and glowing.

During the experience of happiness, some persons felt alert, attentive, and receptive. Their bodies were energetic and full of life. They reported that pleasure had increased and that they radiated life. A sense of completeness and unity pervaded their being. They felt self-confident, optimistic, buoyant, invigorated, enthusiastic, and exuberant. Others felt tranquil, reposed, more peaceful, leisurely, and at ease. There was an inner stillness that refreshed and rejuvenated. Hearts felt open, glad, and full of delight and wonder.

"Having" Experiences of Happiness

In reflecting on the descriptions of happiness, I discovered that people lived out happiness in a "having," "doing," or "being" manner, or in a combination of all three. The children in the first five grades focused on the experience of happiness as a moment of having. Happiness for these boys and girls was receiving presents. Getting something they wanted or receiving something they liked made them happy. Being given a first bicycle or a pet animal was frequently reported as a happy event.

"Having fun" was also perceived as a happy experience. Playing with pets, having a birthday, going fishing, and playing games or sports were all deemed happy moments, as were going to places where they could have fun, such as the beach, ball game, amusement park, zoo, circus, carnival, or movie theater. Holidays, picnics, parades, and situations that were adventurous or out of the ordinary were seen as fun.

Eating something sweet or tasty was also described as a moment of happiness. Ice cream cones, chocolate candy, pizza, hot dogs, brownies, and Big Macs are some of the foods that seem to cause happiness.

Although being loved and having friends were also mentioned by this age group as bringing about happiness, they were not the most frequently described experiences. When they were reported, having a best friend, being with a significant other, being loved by both parents, and being with the family were the situations that fostered happiness.

Many adults reported that their main access to the experience of happiness was through moments of having. A number of men and women implicitly or explicitly sought to possess the psychic good of heightened awareness, mind expansion, will to power, effortless gratification, enlightenment, pure sensibility in the now, or instant inner peace. Some sought moments of happiness through instant transcendence, mastery and control over self, a high level of consciousness, or total self-realization. Experiences that helped people to escape an oppressive sense of problems, emptiness, or boredom were also moments of happiness. Situations in which people experienced being recognized, remembered, appreciated, complimented, accepted, loved, or understood fostered a feeling of happiness, as did being smiled at, listened to, chosen, trusted, or needed.

"Doing" Experiences of Happiness

Although achieving success was connected with happiness in the first graders' descriptions, proving oneself by successful accomplishment became more important as children grew older and became teenagers. Learning to ride a bicycle, drive a car, bake a cake, or play a musical instrument were moments of happiness for some. Making a team, gaining prestige, winning, producing good results, and achieving good grades all pointed to the experience of being able to perform well. "I am able to" experiences seem to give people happiness.

My respondents' descriptions revealed that in order to be happy, men and women must feel safe, secure, and adequate. Feeling approved of and accepted by others helps people to feel secure. But the descriptions indicated that self-acceptance for many came only by proving that they were successful. Doing became their key to success and ultimately to the feeling of happiness.

The descriptions from the adult group seemed to accent this path to happiness. For many individuals happiness came from inflating their egos by striving for power, domination, wealth, authority, status, or the acquisition of knowledge.

"Being" Experiences of Happiness

Happiness also disclosed itself in descriptions of people being with themselves, others, nature, and their God. When respondents were not rushing around hectically or not caught up in worrying about this problem or that responsibility, they reported feeling consistent and congenial with their real self and experiencing a sense of being "at home" with themselves. While taking a walk, doing the dishes, or leisurely "doing nothing," people reported being centered within themselves, comfortable and secure with who they were to the point that they felt a sense of peace, intimacy, and happiness. In these experiences men and women were able simply to be present to themselves in the moment.

Happiness also emerged in experiences of being with others. Sharing space and time with friends, family, and relatives fostered a sense of togetherness and happiness. Enjoying themselves with others at weddings, family reunions, or any celebration, for that matter, were happy experiences for many.

Happiness was sometimes described as being "for" others. In various situations of helping, caring for, sharing with, giving to, and loving others, happiness welled up in many persons.

Absorbing the beauty of nature opened some individuals to a moment of happiness. Flowers, butterflies, the ocean, and mountains invited men and women to "let go" of their anxieties and masks, and simply be with the healing aspects of nature. Hearing birds sing in the morning or arising to a day filled with sunshine woke some people to a moment of happiness.

Resting in the presence of God was also a happy experience. Some persons reported that in believing that the Lord was taking care of them, they were able to relinquish their fears, feel more secure in his presence, and thus, feel happy.

My respondents' descriptions reveal that experiences of having, doing, and being can contribute to the emergence of happiness. The process of inner peace integrates all three of these important areas of human experience. In being grounded in the vital bodily dimension of our existence, we are able to acknowledge that our bodily needs are important and that we should attend to and satisfy them in an appropriate manner. The descriptions of happiness also point to the need to be open to the personal psychological dimension of our existence. Within this domain of experience, we need to fulfill our longings to feel accepted and loved by others, and to develop skills to socialize, adapt, and function as adequate, secure human beings. The transcendent dimension of experience, where we go beyond the vital bodily aspect and the personal "doing" aspect of our existence, was also included in the descriptions of happiness. Living from the dimension of our need to simply *be* is important for our everyday lives.

If we concentrate on a certain dimension of our existence to the neglect of others, we will not grow into living from a sense of inner peace. Happiness experienced in only one dimension will not foster the process of becoming a peace-filled person.

Happiness and Sacred Scripture

After becoming familiar with how people describe their experiences of happiness, I moved into researching how Scripture describes this phenomenon. Matthew Fox, in his book *Breakthrough: Meister Eckhart's Creation Spirituality in New Translation,* [1] points out that creation is God's blessing. It is a gift that enables us to have pleasure and to satisfy the vital bodily dimension of our existence.

In the book of Genesis the authors describe how as the Creator, God designed and organized a world for us in which to live and be with him. [2] He formed and built a place to share his life with us. The Creator imparted vital power to us: he gave something of his spirit to us, and this spirit animates our souls. He keeps his creatures alive and guides them toward himself.

Creation as God's blessing also indicates that God is our creator and master. We are subject to him. He is the source of our lives, and we are called to live according to his way. But it is not easy to surrender to the fact that we are not the origin of our lives. It is a struggle to remain truthful with ourselves and to remember that all is from God. He called us into being out of nothingness. We are wholly dependent upon God's goodness for our survival.

---

1. Matthew Fox, *Breakthrough: Meister Eckhart's Creation Spirituality in New Translation* (Garden City, N.Y.: Doubleday, 1980).

2. Scripture quotes are taken from *The Oxford Annotated Bible,* revised standard version (New York: Oxford University Press, 1962) unless otherwise specified.

The Genesis story reminds us that we have been commissioned by the Creator to continue the process of creation. As creatures we are called to accomplish the work God has given us. The Creator invites us to be his servants and to accept the duty and responsibility to develop our personal-functional dimension of existence. Within this level of experience we are asked by the Creator to continue his work of creation by transforming and humanizing ourselves and all creation.

As creatures we are summoned to cultivate the sacred gift that we are. But we are not each beings unto ourselves. We are all part of creation. To cultivate the sacred gift that we are means also to cultivate the sacred gifts that we are to one another. It is within this personal-functional level of existence that we are empowered to perfect the process of creation.

However, God is not expecting that we perfect creation by ourselves. Happiness is the realization that God is our Shepherd and Light. As he passes life on to us, he remains with us as provider, protector, and sustainer. In Matthew 6:25-34 God invites us to trust in his divine providence. He reassures us not to be anxious for tomorrow, for he will continue to embrace us and watch over us. We need to trust that the Creator wil go on pouring out his goodness, compassion, kindness, mercy, and generosity. His everlasting love will always be present in his constant care of us. Happy are we who remember how vulnerable we are in our creatureliness and have faith and trust that God will continue to be there for us.

In the Wisdom Literature happiness is knowing our place in creation. Scripture invites us to surrender all our self-created security and to realize that we are totally dependent upon God. We need to accept the natural poverty of our humanness and our need for God in our everyday lives.

The author of the Book of Proverbs proclaims: "Happy is the man who finds wisdom and gets understanding" (Prov. 3:13). Wisdom brings peace, happiness, and the abundant life. As we continue to trust in God we grow in wisdom. In remembering to

place our confidence in God and believe in his eternal faithfulness to us, we acquire more wisdom and thus happiness and peace of mind.

The fear of God is described in the Old Testament as the beginning of knowledge and wisdom.[3] To experience the fear of God is to know the immediate reality of God's presence in our lives by way of his acts and manifestations. In order to experience God we must be able to see and hear him. This we do when we behold the wonder of creation.

As we become more open, more able to participate in and respond to the reality of creation, we are able to grow deeper in the experience of the fear of God. In and through the glory of creation we experience a visible manifestation of God and begin to take him seriously. The power and majesty of God are disclosed in the awe and wonder of a sunrise, a sunset, the growth of a plant, or an infant crying in our arms. All these creations of God proclaim his living reality and bring us back to the fundamental truth that apart from God we are nothing. All creation helps us to remember the paramount importance of God. Any dimension of creation re-presents God and proclaims his glory.

Within the fear-of-God experience evoked by becoming awakened to the reality of creation, we begin to reverence God's authorship. Dwelling within the deeper dimension of reality, we realize that we are at the mercy of God. In being open to the overpowering vastness of the world of creation around us, we may be brought to a complete halt and invited to give up the project of controlling the uncontrollable in our lives. It should be pointed out that the awesomeness of creation is not only revealed to us through grandeur and beauty but also through terror, rage, depression, anxiety, loneliness, fear, insecurity, and sexual feelings. Through the various accesses to the awesomeness of creation, each of us is invited to recognize and own our inability to be totally in control and in charge of our life, and

---

3. See: Prov. 1:7, Prov. 9:10, Prov. 15:33, Psalm 111:10, and Job 28:28.

thus to take our place as a creature among other creatures. This process of remembering our proper place in creation leads us to the fear of God and to wisdom and happiness.

The Wisdom Literature in the Old Testament shows us that life takes place under a wider horizon than our own narrow interests and concerns. We must go beyond our physical and personal-functional dimensions of existence and enter the transcendent realm. By living from the being dimension of reality, we grow in wisdom and peace. The transcendent dimension of our experience reminds us of the sacredness of reality.

In order to discover the sacredness of all that is, Wisdom Literature instructs us to adopt a certain attitude toward life. From this perspective of keeping holy the things that are holy,[4] we are able to see reality in a new light. Wisdom, inner peace, and happiness mean the ability to look at all things from God's point of view. From Yahweh's perspective, all of reality is his creation. Everything in the world reflects his presence. Wisdom perceives that God is at the root of everything; he is the foundation of existence. His radiance permeates all reality.

Wise persons live from the transcendent perspective of reality and are committed to life as sacred. Such men and women seek to encounter sacredness in all people, events, and things. Awe, wonder, and the fear of God open them to a perspective from which they begin to sense the transcendent in the common and simple. In revering Yahweh's creation, they surrender to their own fragile, vulnerable selves and their basic poverty of being.

Wise persons know their place in creation and are able to adopt a proper attitude toward the universe. They begin to see their lives in light of the dimension of eternity. From this perspective, wise men and women develop a more workable attitude toward life as a whole. The meaning of their place in the world is disclosed, and they begin to accept the world and life as they are.

---

4. Book of Wisdom 6:10; Scripture reference taken from *The Jerusalem Bible,* reader's edition (Garden City, N.Y.: Doubleday, 1971).

In this acceptance, such wise persons own their weakness, limitedness, and need for God. In the Wisdom Literature of the Old Testament happiness is the process of coming to live peacefully, which grows out of a need for God in everyday life.

The New Testament is also helpful in understanding the experience of happiness. Here, in the Gospel of John, we learn Christ's promise of peace: "Peace is my farewell to you. My peace is my gift to you and I do not give it to you as the world gives it. Do not let your hearts be troubled, and do not be fearful."[5] Peace is a gift that Jesus gives to us. Scripture scholar Raymond Brown comments on this passage:

> The peace of which Jesus speaks has nothing to do with the absence of warfare . . . nor with an end to psychological tension, nor with a sentimental feeling of well being . . . In Johannine language "peace," "truth," "light," "life," and "joy" are figurative terms reflecting different facets of the great gift that Jesus has brought from the Father to men. "Peace is my gift to you" is another way of saying "I give them eternal life."[6]

The message of the New Testament and specifically of John's gospel is that we need the Son of Man for the fulfillment of our lives. Christ does not offer us happiness, but he does offer us the promise of life, a new life of the spirit. He invites us to share in the living presence of the divine life, to live life more fully (John 10:10).

If we are alive to our inner uneasiness we may discover that we are hungry for a deeper, richer life. We realize that the physical and the personal-functional dimensions of human existence are not enough. Flowing with the pleasure principle in an appropriate manner and allowing our impulse life to inform us of our vital bodily needs can foster the process of becoming truly human. But the restlessness in our bodies speaks to us about a need for something more. On the personal-functional level of

---

5. Scripture quote taken from Raymond Brown, *The Gospel According to John XIII-XXI* (Garden City, N.Y.: Doubleday, 1970), p. 649.
6. Ibid., p. 653.

existence we are called to live according to the reality principle. It is important to build a secure identity for ourselves, to gain a sense of social maturity, and to manage and control the world around us. But deep within us there is a pull to go beyond the personal-functional dimension. On the transcendent level of existence our beings long to be filled. They hunger and thirst for something more.

The Gospel of John calls us to cultivate an intimate relationship with God, the source of our life, love, and peace. In this sense intimacy is the process of growing into a knowledge of God. We come to know God through Jesus, his Son. He invites us to believe and see that he is the Word of God. The believing, seeing, and knowing to which Jesus leads us are rooted in the experience of the heart.

John's gospel calls us to an interior transformation, that of knowing Jesus with our whole heart. This means that we are attentive to Jesus and seek him out as he reveals himself to us in our everyday lives. The Son of God cautions us: "Let not your hearts be troubled; believe in God, believe also in me" (John 14:1). Out of our inner springs of faith we enter into a personal relationship with God. We come to know the Son of God by participating in his life and living from our transcendent dimension. It is in living from the hunger for the "more than" that we are motivated to continue to seek intimacy with Jesus. Peace emerges in sharing an intimate relationship with the Son of God.

The transformation of our interior being results from recognizing Jesus as our Shepherd, who gently opens the gate to the Father. Jesus is the Way, the Truth, and the Life; no one comes to the Father but by him (John 14:6). We are his little children; he will not leave us orphans. Jesus is aware of our vulnerability. He is our light of hope who promises to nourish and sustain us. The Gospel of John calls us to continue to be children of God. As children our hearts are soft, open, humble, innocent, and filled with wonder. A child is well aware of its dependence on others. The new covenant calls us to trust in God and in Jesus. We need to look for Jesus in our everyday lives, and to follow his way. He reassures us not to be afraid, for he is with us always. He is our security, our strength, and our peace. In offering us his life, he invites us into a new creation of ourselves.

In order to be recreated, to be born anew, we must grow in faith and in love. The Gentile military officer (John 4:46-54) and the cripple at Bethzatha (John 5:1-24) are examples of people who have faith and love in Jesus and his Father. They are both humbly receptive to Jesus. Both men acknowledge and declare in response to Jesus' presence that they are in need. They desire to be helped and to be restored to wholeness and peace. These men are able to hear the Word of God, to reach out and ask him for a rebirth, a new creation. They do not rely on their egoism; rather, they choose to become God-reliant. The presence of Jesus draws them out of their self-sufficient attitude. They recognize that they cannot achieve wholeness and peace with their own willpower.

The stories of both men also indicate that rebirth is just the beginning of the invitation to grow in intimacy, wholeness, and inner peace with the Son of God. As with the cripple, we must carry our own bed and make our own way. Jesus will show us the light and give us his life, but we must desire to walk with him. We are responsible for keeping our hearts empty in order to have space to welcome him into our lives.

Obstacle to Peace

In reflecting upon my everyday experience, I may begin to see that an obstacle to peace within me emerges from my sense of insecurity and my way of dealing with it. Typically, this insecurity is obvious neither to others nor to myself. It even seems normal. That is, most people around me probably live their lives fundamentally motivated by this veiled sense of insecurity.

As I consider my experience, I come to understand that this fundamental insecurity within me seems to harden my heart and to prevent my growing into a more intimate relationship with my self and my God. Controlled by this subtle insecurity, my consciousness becomes clouded, distracted, and closed. Because of this hardness of heart, I am unable to comprehend and believe in the Word and thus unable to grow in his peace. I may listen but I do not understand. Perceiving the deeper meanings of what is there before me becomes an almost impossible task.

Need for Love and Acceptance

Reflecting upon my experience, I come in touch with my need to be accepted and loved so that I can feel at peace, at home, and comfortable with myself. From this atmosphere of security, I am able to accept things as they are. I accept my personal limitations and weaknesses as part of me. I feel at peace with the truth of who I am. With this attitude, I am able to see and hear the Word of God. My heart is open and receptive to being moved, touched, and transformed.

The childhood residue of being loved and accepted in an imperfect way still exists within me. From my reading of Scripture, I realize that only my Creator has the power to love and accept me perfectly. I must admit to myself that through no fault of theirs, my parents and teachers and the other significant persons in my life were naturally imperfect in their care and love for me. Because of this background of imperfect love and acceptance, my existence is permeated with subtle feelings of being loved and accepted in an imperfect way. I have never been and will never be totally loved and totally accepted for who I am. Only God can bless me with that experience. Being the finite, limited creature that I am, I struggle with wanting more love and more acceptance from the imperfect others around me. In the natural need of wanting more I may be tempted to strive and to compete for more love and acceptance.

During moments of insecurity I realize my need for more secure ground on which to stand. My search for this firm ground may lead me to seek the approval of another, to have my ego massaged and proclaimed acceptable. Because the residual vulnerability from my childhood has been carried over into my adult life, I may experience moments of inferiority, inadequacy, and fear of failure.

Seeking Approval of Others

My insecurity may lead me to seek the approval of others. I may feel that their approval will be forthcoming if I live up to their expectations. So I begin to feel that I must perform well. Self-doubt and feelings of inadequacy well up within me. The assumed expectations of the other become my measuring stick. I continue to lay more expectations on myself; in order to be loved and accepted, I must live up to the ideal. My consciousness becomes preoccupied with seeking the praise and recognition of the other, with "doing." Anxiety, insecurity, inadequacy, and self-doubt choke my ability to be open to the deeper dimension of reality. I become preoccupied with building up my life on a base of false securities. My intense involvement with worldly cares fulfills my need to be secure.

The culture tells me that if I am successful I will be respected and people will pay attention to me. This recognition may temporarily satisfy those unmet needs from my childhood. However, success is only a moment. If I am to continue to achieve success and feel falsely secure, I will become driven to live out, not moments of success, but a style of success. I will then have built my own trap. If I do not win, I lose. In our culture, the act of losing is perceived as failure. I do not want to lose, and thus fail.

My residual childhood insecurity impels me to win, to become number one in order to attain a sense of self-worth. The need to succeed and avoid failure causes all kinds of tensions that slowly harden my heart.

My insecurity can lead me to try constantly to please others. I may become caught up in the fear that others do not perceive me as good enough. Perfection becomes my goal. If I am perfect, I will win. People will respect me. They will approve of me, and love me.

In striving to have others think well of me, I may become ruled by my plans, projects, schedules, and duties. I compulsively crowd my schedule with things I must do for others. Time becomes tight. My duties continue to demand more and more. There is never enough time to finish one task before another intrudes.

If I am fortunate enough to remain in touch with my experience, I may be able to see my residual childhood insecurity for what it is: the demon in my life. This fundamental insecurity can control my life and harden my heart.

Through the gentle activity of reflecting upon my daily experience, I may realize that in coping with my insecurity I have become too self-sufficient. I have forgotten that I am utterly dependent upon God and that I am sustained by the breath of his spirit. In my self-sufficient style, I forget that without God, I can do nothing.

Need to Empty Self

In the Gospel of Mark we hear the story of the rich man.

And Jesus looking upon him loved him and said to him, "You lack one thing; go, sell what you have, and give to the poor, and you will have treasure in heaven; and come, follow me." At that saying his countenance fell, and he went away sorrowful; for he had great possessions. And Jesus looked around and said to his disciples, "How hard it will be for those who have riches to enter the kingdom of God." And the disciples were amazed at his words. But Jesus said to them again, "Children, how hard it is to enter the kingdom of God. It is easier for a camel to go through the eye of a needle than for a rich man to enter the kingdom of God." (Mark 10:21-26)

The author seems to be telling me that God wants all of me, whole and entire. Because of my insecurity, I have become preoccupied with surviving and with developing a self-sufficient attitude. I do not submit to God, but rather try to survive on my own. "*I will* do it" becomes my motto. *I will* get the love and attention I need. *I will* make myself secure in this life. *I will* acquire status, success, power, and possessions—whatever I need to give myself a sense of security.

In pausing to get in touch with my experience, I discover that this drive to acquire a sense of security is a drive to build an untrue sense of self. Unknowingly, I am holding on to my misleading sense of security in a quiet, desperate way. I cannot face the truth that I am not the source of my life. My false sense of self helps me to participate in a process of self-deception, which tells me that I am power and glory.

In the story of the rich man, Jesus calls me to give up my riches: my false sense of self. In my self-sufficient manner, I have built up a kingdom of success, of security, of power. In my kingdom, I possess the respect of others. They accept me and therefore I feel good; I feel like a rich man in control of his life.

The Gospel of Mark invites me to let go of my false self, of my false sense of security and control. In Mark 8:34-36, the author describes how Jesus called the multitude and said to them: "If any man would come after me, let him deny himself and take up his cross and follow me. For whoever would save his life will lose it and whoever loses his life for my sake and the gospel's will save it. For what does it profit a man, to gain the whole world and forfeit his life?"

The art of reflective living calls me out of my constant striving to build my kingdom of honor and glory, where I am secure. I see my life more clearly, for reflection puts distance between me and my everyday struggle to deal with my insecurity.

Meditating on Sacred Scripture, I begin to understand the story of the rich man in Mark's gospel. I realize that Christ calls me to empty myself of the inward noise and hecticness that flow from building my kingdom of security. I need to let go of my controlling, self-sufficient attitude. Giving up my riches means giving up the security that I have worked so hard to acquire. My riches have become my defense against my insecurity; gaining security has become my ultimate project. But this false security has shut me off from others and God.

Mark 8:34-36 calls me to deny myself. In listening to my heart, I uncover the self I need to give up. Lost in the process of constructing my false security, I have been caught up with worrying about what others will think of me. I have become attached to my self-will. Doing has been my most important defense. As long as I was doing, I was in control, striving to build my self-image of success.

Pausing so as to distance myself from my workaday world, I am able to reflect on my behavior. I see that my life has been cluttered, a result of my ego's constant quest for security. My weakness has been my inclination to self-centeredness and hardness of heart. The demon in me that I have discovered in my moments of reflection is my inclination to build my kingdom of security by working hard to please others, so that they will offer me praise, recognition, acceptance, and love.

Sacred Scripture calls me to transform my heart, to soften it so that it may receive the Word of God. With a gentle, humble heart, I am able to believe and trust that God will take care of me. I need to let go of building my own kingdom and trust that the Lord will sustain me and be my ground of security.

Conclusion

The New Testament is a story of how the Father and Son love us. The new covenant is an invitation to grow in inner peace by loving one another as Jesus loves us (John 13:34). But in order to love another, we must first love ourselves. The interior transformation that Jesus asks of us is rooted in the process of meeting ourselves, accepting ourselves, and appreciating ourselves as children of God, that is, of growing into a deeper acknowledgment of who we truly are. The presence of Jesus helps us to own and claim our limitedness, our smallness, and our powerlessness. In knowing who we are, we experience our humble place in God's creation. We need to embrace our creaturehood and love and abide in who we are.

In loving ourselves, we begin to know how the Father and Son abide in us. With open and receptive hearts, we can believe that the Father and Son love us and are calling us to abide in their love. Rooted in a love for ourselves, and a love for the Father and Son, we are able to venture forth and live out this love by giving it to one another as Jesus gave his love to us. To transform our lives into a God-consciousness is to grow in intimacy, love, and inner peace with ourselves, the Father and Son, and with one another.

Audrey E. Campbell-Wray, Ph.D. (cand.), is ancillary therapies director at the House of Affirmation in Montara, California. In this capacity, she directs the art therapy, spirituality, and activities programs. Ms. Campbell-Wray brings to the House of Affirmation the richness of her Afro-American culture and a varied educational and experiential background. A native New Yorker, she attended Hunter College before completing a tour of duty with the U.S. Navy as a neuropsychiatric technician. She subsequently received an undergraduate degree in fine arts and psychology from Lone Mountain College, San Francisco; a master's degree in theology from St. John's University, New York; and a master's degree in applied spirituality from the University of San Francisco. Currently Ms. Campbell-Wray is pursuing doctoral studies in clinical psychology at the Psychological Studies Institute in Palo Alto, California. She is a member of the American Art Therapy Association, the American Society of Group Psychotherapy and Psychodrama, and the International Society of Artists.

The Forgotten Tree: An Invitation to Happiness

Audrey E. Campbell-Wray

I have constructed my discussion of happiness in the form of a circle: the circle begins with a scriptural reflection on the tree of life as an invitation to live forever in union with God. It continues with a reflection on life energy in terms of wholeness and affirmation; consciousness and vision; creativity and the struggle with death; and vulnerability, mysticism, and joy. The circle comes around with a discussion of form and art, not in terms of specific disciplines, but in terms of belief systems, relationships, and breakthroughs.

> Out of the ground the Lord God made various trees grow that were delightful to look at and good for food, with the tree of life in the middle of the garden and the tree of the knowledge of good and bad. (Gen. 2:9)

> Then the Lord God said: "See! The man has become like one of us, knowing what is good and what is bad! Therefore, he must not be allowed to put out his hand to take fruit from the tree of life also, and thus eat of it and live forever." (Gen. 3:22)

> The angel then showed me the river of life-giving water, clear as crystal, which issued from the throne of God and of the Lamb and flowed down the middle of the streets. On either side of the river grew the trees of life which produce fruit twelve times a year, once each month; their leaves serve as medicine for the nations. Nothing deserving a curse shall be found there. The throne of God and of the Lamb shall be there, and his servants shall serve him faithfully. They shall see him face to face and bear his name on their foreheads. The

107

night shall be no more. They will need no light from lamps or the sun, for the Lord God shall give them light, and they shall reign forever. (Rev. 22:1-4)

Happy are they who wash their robes so as to have free access to the tree of life and enter the city through its gates! (Rev. 22:14)[1]

I

False belief: We have lost access to the tree of life. Therefore we are prone to function as if the Messiah had never really come, or as if we have examined the gift of salvation and found it wanting.

False belief: Real power resides in sin. We are inclined, therefore, to act on the belief that badness and evil are imbued with more power, and that love is weak and powerless.

False belief: Christians are called to seek pain, to reject happiness. "Am I happy?" is not a permissible question.

False belief: There is no joy.

With the tree of life in the middle of the Garden, where it has always been, and the accomplished work of the Messiah, we can reflect with the Johannine writings on the immediacy of our access to life. We have a realized eschatology, a passage through death to life. Jesus penetrates the depths of our sin and raises us to the heights of glory at one and the same time. That simultaneity reflects the paradox with which we all must cope. Living requires us to deal with whatever it presents. We are redeemed now, loved now, happy now, joyful now. We are in pain now, in illness now, in feelings now, even in death now. Death and resurrection are current and simultaneous. The effects of the tree of good and evil are transcended and we may walk and sit together in the Garden today, and dine on the fruit of the tree of life today, and with all that is, be happy. The

---

1. Scriptural quotes are taken from *New American Bible,* Saint Joseph Edition (New York: Catholic Book Publishing, 1970).

going-to-be-when mentality nourishes a particular passion for never experiencing ourselves as enough—today. No one is going to be transformed into someone next year that she or he is not already—today. "Today you will be with me" is the wisdom of the Now.

II

The affirmation of life is the process of directing energy into wholeness and expanding that energy. Consciousness can be characterized as expanding energy. The emotions as heaters, movers, and expanders release energy and can move us through fire. Consciousness as both reason and intuition spans both science and mysticism. We resist expansion of consciousness by our conservative conceptual style of dealing with life. We think in terms of belief systems that as often as not close us to possibilities. As soon as our belief systems exclude, definitively define, segregate, stereotype, or present us with more shoulds and can'ts than maybes, we engulf ourselves in limits and proceed to function as if those limits are the whole of truth, being, and life. Robert Ornstein addresses this kind of thinking in his work *The Psychology of Consciousness.*

> We all seem to set limits on possibility and to work within these assumed limits. . . . We screen out much of our surroundings because we do not believe that certain events occur. Once a friend unwittingly emphasized this to me by reversing an ordinary saying: "I'll see it when I believe it!" If an object or sensory input appears which does not fit our set of categories, we may ignore it.[2]

> We are often unaware of the full effect of our tools, be they physical instruments or doctrines such as behaviorism. We often imagine that tools, like sensory organs, serve exclusively to extend awareness, but in fact we are wrong. Both serve to limit as well as extend. Abraham Maslow, commenting on the effects of a strict behaviorism in psychology, said, "If the only

---

2. Robert E. Ornstein, *The Psychology of Consciousness* (New York: Penguin Books, 1972), p. 18.

tool you have is a hammer, you tend to treat everything as if it were a nail." A corrective needs to be applied.[3]

In theological terms, expanded consciousness can be called vision: a belief system opened to the possibilities it implies, promises, and even demonstrates.

Jesus expanded his being. His energy is free, subtle, and mystical. It spreads his gravitational pull and he walks on water. Peter is captured by the vision, the possibility. Peter walks on water. Inhibition freezes the emotional heaters, reduces the vision, paralyzes the energy. We are like Peter when, filled with inhibition and fear, we turn to ask, "Are you lying to me?" and fall into the water.

We fall into the water somewhat blinded and enter the endless cycle of problems and questions to which we will not admit possibilities or solutions. It is a neurotic bind and a continual reconsideration of the problems and the questions. The pain prods us. It is an impetus to grow. We are prodded to try to remember who we really are, to find form in the chaos. The ability to find form in chaos, to get unstuck, unfrozen, to put things together as we have never known them before—that is creativity. Creativity offers a solution to the neurotic bind. As Rollo May points out in *The Courage to Create:*

> The creative process must be explored not as the product of sickness, but as representing the highest degree of emotional health, as the expression of the normal people in the act of actualizing themselves. Creativity must be seen in the work of the scientist as well as in that of the artist, in the thinker as well as in the aesthetician; and one must not rule out the extent to which it is present in captains of modern technology as well as in a mother's normal relationship with her child. Creativity, as Webster rightly indicates, is basically the process of making, of bringing into being.[4]
> . . . .

3. Ibid., p. 23.

4. Rollo May, *The Courage to Create* (New York: W. W. Norton, 1975), pp. 33-34.

The creative process is the expression of this passion for form. It is the struggle against disintegration, the struggle to bring into existence new kinds of being that give harmony and integration.[5]

The painful prod may very well be the poison within, a shadow repository of psychic refuse, deprivations, and traumas. The next stage is to work through these psychic remnants, not hate or disown them, not freeze or inhibit them. Both meditation and psychotherapy ought to offer a creative solution to the neurotic bind and enable us to live more under the light of eternity. They ought to enable us to reach out and touch the tree of life in the middle of the Garden. They do this by providing a glimpse of the possibilities, or a vision of the whole, now, and by confronting us with death. Out of the struggle with death (not death itself), creativity is born, Beauty is born!

III

The way of art is beauty—not as appearance but as wholeness. Wholeness—not in isolation but in relationship. Relationship—not as rigid concepts but as mysticism and vulnerability. The way of art is open to eternity, open to possibilities. The way of art does not require ease and smoothness. It thrives best when one is vulnerable and dry. A little brokenness does not hinder; as Hereclitus knew, "Dry souls are best." Then a mere glimpse of beauty, a brief burning touch of wholeness, an echo or reflection of the sacred can enter like a raging torrent. Breakthrough. The vulnerability is an act of seeking, praying, creating, now: allowing the mystical embracing of one another in loving awareness.

We can live as if the tree of life is indeed available to us—restored by a supreme act of love. We can trust.

Master, speak. You need not come. Your word is enough. Your word is sufficient.

---

5. Ibid., p. 146.

Reverend John A. Struzzo, C.S.C., Ph.D., is a full-time psychotherapist at the House of Affirmation in Montara, California. A priest of the Congregation of Holy Cross, Father Struzzo received his bachelor's and master's degrees in theology and sociology at the University of Notre Dame and his doctorate in sociology from Florida State University. For several years Father Struzzo was Professor of Sociology at Northern Illinois University. He then completed a postgraduate certificate in marriage and family psychotherapy at the Institute of Religion and Health in New York City, and interned in clinical psychology at Worcester State Hospital. Before joining the staff of the House of Affirmation, Father Struzzo was executive director of a pastoral counseling center in South Bend, Indiana. He has lectured widely on issues relating to psychology and religion, and on personal growth and development. He is a member of the American Association of Pastoral Counselors, the American Association of Marriage and Family Therapists, and the California Association of Marriage and Family Therapy.

Happiness: A Developmental Perspective

John A. Struzzo

There is a story told of Tolstoy that as he was walking in a forest, he met a lizard. "Your heart is beating," he said, "the sun is shining; you're happy." Then after a pause he added, "I'm not."[1] In his *Varieties of Religious Experience,* William James comments that Goethe, despite the optimism in his writings, claimed to have experienced only four weeks of genuine well-being in his entire life.[2] Thoreau asserts that all human beings live lives of quiet desperation. If I were to ask you, "Are you happy?" I would probably get such responses as, "I don't feel unhappy," or "I do feel somewhat depressed." However, implicit in each answer is an assumption about what happiness means. For some people happiness is the absence of pain or the feeling of pleasure. For others it may mean the achievement of some goal and the concomitant feelings. I would like to suggest that happiness has different meanings according to one's stage of psychospiritual development.

Four broad stages of psychospiritual development challenge the adult: (1) the fulfillment of basic needs—primarily security,

---

1. John S. Dunne, *The Way of All the Earth* (New York: Macmillan, 1972), p. 27. Many of the ideas in this article have been inspired by John Dunne's writings and my conversations with him.

2. William James, *Varieties of Religious Experience* (New York: Random House, 1936), p. 135.

113

sexuality, and power; (2) "letting go" and "waiting for"; (3) insight; and (4) interdependence and integration. I will discuss the task of each stage and the ensuing process that seems to be related to happiness.

Needs Fulfillment

Most people focus their energy on the fulfillment of their basic needs, assuming that if they get enough security, sexual fulfillment, and power, they will be happy. Happiness is perceived to be outside of oneself; others are expected to fulfill these basic needs.

Security

A preoccupation with self-preservation occupies the lowest level of needs. At this level we are constantly afraid of being injured, or experience a strong desire to hurt or injure others. We tend to experience a global anxiety, which at root is the fear of annihilation—a fear of death. Sometimes these fears are projected onto others, and a person then experiences paranoia. Thus one might perceive oneself as kind and caring, and see others as the source of threat. The basic question becomes, "How can I feel secure in the face of such fears?"

Behaviorally, we defend against fear by gearing up for a "fight or flight" response—the body becomes ready either to attack the enemy, whether real or imagined, or to flee. It is like driving a car with one foot on the brake and the other foot on the gas. When confronted by an overwhelming threat of pain that cannot be countered by either flight or fight, we tend to feel panic or rage. If we try to flee, we do so in blind desperation; if we cannot flee, we feel trapped and enraged. Terror is experienced in the paralysis of the muscular system.

When we feel threatened, we tend to become preoccupied with certitude and may tend to perceive the world in black and white categories. We want clear answers: yes or no; right or wrong. We tend to be especially preoccupied with law-and-order issues. In interpersonal relationships, we constantly look for reassurance in the other's approval. To experience happiness at this stage of development, we need to feel a basic security. We need to feel protected and safe from abandonment, and to experience constancy and predictability in our life.

Sensate Needs

Once we feel a basic security, a higher level of need emerges, and we begin to focus energy on sensate pleasures, especially sexual ones. There is a preoccupation with physical pleasures and sexual release. Involvement in sexual acts does not necessarily indicate a focus at this stage, however, for such acts could also be signs of power, love, or other motivation. At this level of need, other people and oneself tend to be perceived as sexual objects. Since physical pleasure, especially sexual, is a central preoccupation, a person's whole life is affected: clothes, hairstyle, manner of speaking, car, home. In general, one's presentation of self is sexualized and geared for sexual conquest, or avoidance of sexual desire: desire and aversion are two sides of the same coin.

The ability to experience pleasure is a sustaining creative force in our lives. Alexander Lowen has argued that "underlying any experience . . . of happiness is a bodily sensation of pleasure."[3] In order to experience pleasure we must let go of the body— allow the body to respond freely. The greatest obstacle to experiencing pleasure is disassociation from our bodies. Once we have blocked an awareness of our bodies, we tend to feel empty, lifeless. If, for example, a man cannot feel his legs, he will be emotionally insecure because he will feel that his legs cannot hold him up—that he is not grounded. The ability to experience pleasure, then, is both a reinforcement of the feeling of security and the prerequisite for the enjoyment of happiness.

Power

Once we feel sufficient satisfaction of the need for pleasure, a higher level of need arises: power. At this stage we are primarily

---

3. Alexander Lowen, *Pleasure* (New York: Lancer Books, 1970), p. 24.

preoccupied with domination and submission. Life becomes a power struggle—a zero-sum game in which winning means the opponent must lose. We manifest our preoccupation with control in our constant desire to change others and ourselves. Thus, if I am standing in line at the grocery store and feel irritated with the cashier for being so slow, I am experiencing the desire to change her, and therefore control her. My striving for control is also revealed when, for example, I become impatient with traffic lights while driving. If I feel anger at myself for my limitations or weaknesses, then I am trying to control myself. All of these examples illustrate a preoccupation with power. Because we feel afraid, resentful, angry, and jealous, we tend to feel critical and judgmental of ourselves and others. Our energy is devoted to survival. It is we against the world.

Have you ever been feeling peaceful and then suddenly become irritated when someone enters the room? The person who comes into the room seemingly has done nothing but share the same space with you. Yet you are intuitively aware that he is an angry person. His very presence seems to spread a negative energy across the room. Negativity begets negativity. You then begin to feel resistance and your own anger. When we actively strive for power, we tend to create fear and anger in others. The root of anger is a feeling of powerlessness.

During a power struggle, we feel that we are right and the other is wrong. Consequently, we tend to be defensive and self-righteous, which creates an escalating resistance in the opponent. Whatever the original question was, it becomes irrelevant. The issue now is, who is going to make the rules here, and how can I win?

To be able to experience a sense of control over my life and others is essential for a sense of self-esteem and for happiness. Without the ability to be self-assertive, I cannot love either myself or others. Without self-affirmation, the striving for power becomes aggression and violence. To be self-affirming means to be able to defend my dignity, rights, and beliefs.

Frustration and Disappointment

At the stage of need fulfillment, we experience security, sensate pleasure, and power as gratifying and, therefore, conducive to happiness. At the same time, we feel a sense of unfulfillment and begin to believe that if we could only recapture those initial feelings, happiness would follow. Consequently, we almost compulsively repeat earlier experiences in an attempt to gain more security, sensate pleasure, and power. Although at times this process brings momentary relief, we also feel a certain emptiness. We eventually realize that the search is endless, and fear, anxiety, and sometimes depression ensue. At this point, we are presented with an opportunity for change. However, the ego always reacts defensively to change, for its attachments and aversions are integral parts of our self-image. For change to happen we must accept the painful experience of disappointment and frustration of our striving and wants. What before was a source of happiness no longer satisfies, and we feel unhappy.

Letting Go

It is not that security, sensate pleasure, and power in themselves create unhappiness. Rather, it is the internal addiction, the striving and grasping, that creates unhappiness. An addiction is basically an attachment to a sensation, object, or person, such that we become increasingly dependent on it as a main source of gratification. The more we strive for gratification, the more we feel unsatisfied, and the more intense the craving becomes. Unhappiness is rooted in the grasping, the desire for fulfillment, and the inability to be fulfilled. Happiness, then, is the unclenching of our grasp—the letting go of the attachment. We do not let go of security, sensate pleasure, or power, but the wanting, the inner striving, the grasping. Ultimately it means the letting go of the "not having."

Only after we encounter frustration will we let go and unclench our grasp. Letting go becomes a consent to unfulfillment.

We then enter the void, and let the void be void. We relinquish control over our life and allow ourself to be led.

At this point, the quest for fulfillment shifts to a quest for wholeness. On the cognitive level, there is a shift from a search for certitude to a search for understanding.

Thus, when we focus our energies on external things and persons with the expectation that they will fulfill our basic needs, we become dependent. Three consequences follow from this dependence on other people. First, we want their approval; otherwise, we feel that we will not get what we want. Consequently, we tend to tailor our responses to what we think others want to hear, or what we think will be pleasing to them. Concomitantly, we resent our allowing them to control us. Second, we want to control them because we are afraid that we will be deprived of what we want. Third, we harbor suppressed anger and hostility, because we realize that these persons have the power to withhold from us. This desire for approval and control underpins our search for fulfillment of basic needs. Happiness demands a letting go of these basic wants. We let go not of the approval or control, but the wanting, the striving. Our letting go does not end the desire, but we attain a new relationship to the desire. Thus saying yes to loneliness does not take away the loneliness, but it does enable wholeness to emerge. Loneliness then becomes transformed into hospitality.

In letting go, we enter into our own inner emptiness. We learn to live the question rather than seek absolute answers and certitude. The immediate experience is often one of anxiety, doubt, confusion, and depression. We feel the pain of deprivation and a quiet desperation. But letting go can be merely a resignation, if there is no ''waiting for.'' To resign oneself can lead to further depression and helplessness and even suicide. To wait for means to discern an unknown path. Psychologically, the inner emptiness may be seen as illness; spiritually, it is an invitation to a journey. Growth demands taking responsibility for the pain and exploring the meaning of it.

Insight

In Arthur Miller's play *After the Fall,* Holga in a recurring dream gives birth to an idiot.[4] The child keeps trying to climb on her lap. She feels horrified and repulsed. Finally, she bends down and kisses the broken face of the child. Growth demands that we continually bring into awareness parts of ourselves that we previously regarded as repulsive and dirty, so they can be integrated. When Holga finally says yes to her dark side, she becomes able to say yes to life.

In the Buddhist scriptures, there is a story of a farmer who grew great crops year after year. He collected manure from his animals and spread it all over the land. Each year the land was restored and the harvest was abundant. Later, a second farmer took over. He found the work revolting and dirty and therefore did not collect the manure. After a few years, his harvest began to dwindle. The crops no longer grew and the soil became sterile.[5]

Similarly, when we repress and refuse to acknowledge parts of ourselves that we are uncomfortable with or find repulsive, we set the stage for a sterile future. Thus if we refuse to acknowledge and experience our anger, we also stifle our passion. We deaden ourselves into a gutless, passionless conformity. The more we refuse to acknowledge and experience our sexuality, whether it be homosexual or heterosexual, the more we suppress our creativity. The more we repress or run away from our loneliness, the more we stifle our potential for hospitality.

Letting go is not a mere resignation but a positive consent to the darkness. Instead of fighting or denying the darkness, we allow ourselves to be led by insight. The darkness itself then shows the way of the unknown path. For example, we learn to

---

4. Arthur Miller, *After the Fall* (New York: Viking Press, 1964), pp. 21f.
5. Swami Rama et al., *Yoga and Psychotherapy* (Honesdale, Penn.: Himalayan International Institute, 1976), p. 230.

sit with loneliness, and by focusing on the feeling, we gradually learn its meaning. In order to explore that meaning we must understand that the language of darkness is one of image, metaphor, and symbol. It is the language of dreams and fantasy. Each insight gained gives direction to the future. Thus we learn to let go of control over life and are open to being led. Light emerges out of the darkness itself. By allowing ourselves to feel our depression, anxiety, rejection, boredom, hurt, anger, sexuality, insecurity, and powerlessness, we make their integration possible. What previously appeared to be our enemy becomes our ally. By acknowledging, taking responsibility for, and experiencing and accepting these feelings, we befriend the darkness. It is there our strength and healing power lies.

Have you ever lighted a fire at night in a forest? The larger the campfire, the more darkness there seems to be. Similarly, the more insight we gain, the more we experience the depths of the darkness.

The Present is Sufficient

In the process of letting go we relinquish the expectation of the fulfillment of our basic needs. We realize that suffering and happiness are not incompatible. Previously we had perceived happiness as the absence of pain, and much of the struggle was to avoid pain, especially the suffering of deprivation. We come to realize, however, that an unhappy loneliness reflects our inner poverty. Happiness is rooted in our inner solitude—our own inner richness. In the process of letting go of the fulfillment of basic needs, we may still prefer to have more security, sensate pleasure, and power, but we also realize that they are not indispensable. Deprivation is now experienced as an opportunity for insight and growth. We also realize that we have everything we need here and now to be happy. When we are grasping and striving, we are bound to the past and future and ignore the here and now.

Let us suppose you meet a woman at a party who strongly attracts you, and you begin to feel you must have her as a friend. The assumption is that you will never be happy until you do.

You begin to focus a lot of energy on trying to befriend her. You look over in her direction, waiting for an opportunity to speak with her alone. Meanwhile others are trying to talk to you. You only half listen, for your attention and energy are focused on this one particular person. Thus you miss out on the here and now possibilities. Now let us suppose that you let go of your striving for her friendship. You then begin to realize that there are other people present who have attractive personalities. You begin to enjoy them and the party. Until now, you felt merely desire and unfulfillment and only a hope for happiness. Unhappiness is the result of focusing on the not having, the deprivation, the unfulfilled desire. In letting go, we get in return all the security, sensate pleasure, and power we need to be happy. Jesus said, "Whoever leaves home or brothers or sisters or mother or father or children or fields . . . will receive a hundredfold in this life" (Mark 10:29-30). However, what we receive may be quite different from what we expected. As long as we are striving for fulfillment, it continually eludes our grasp. The very striving seems to ensure that we do not get what we want.

Ultimately, letting go is to risk death. At the root of our striving and attachments and aversions is the fear of death. For example, I feel I must manipulate you to get your approval. Underneath is the fear of rejection: if I show myself to you as I really am, then you will see that I am no one, and you will not approve of me; you will see that I am dead. Thus I feel the need to defend against that fear and to prevent your seeing my vulnerability. When I risk rejection and allow myself to be vulnerable, I risk appearing empty and unimportant—as no one. In my striving for approval, I place expectations on you. I expect you to like and accept me as a result of my behavior. Thus if I am to let go, I need to forgive you—to release you from those expectations. Instead of focusing on your response to me I need to accept the possibility that you indeed may not like me. I must realize that I do not need your acceptance before I can be happy. Once we realize that things do not have to be a certain way, hope arises.

Although fear tends to push us away from its object, we are also fascinated by what we fear. Underneath fear and aversion is desire for the dreaded object. Thus the fear of sex is in reality a desire for sex. To use one's energy to avoid sex or to repress it is not much different from an addictive desire to gratify sexual needs. Aversion and attachment are two sides of the same coin.

Religious Vows: Example of Letting Go

Similarly, we cannot let go of something we never possessed in the first place. This helps to explain why some religious who take vows of poverty, celibacy, and obedience are miserable. The vows are a good example of the letting go of the striving for security, sensate pleasure, and power. However, if a person has never had these needs satisfied, letting go will be experienced as deprivation rather than wholeness and can lead to a greater obsession and attachment.

Let us first consider celibacy: celibacy is basically a letting go of our striving for sexual fulfillment in its physical manifestation. However, if I try to control sexual energy without first coming to know it, it will turn against me. We cannot destroy sexual energy; we can only transform or release it. If I never come to know and experience it, it will be thrust into the unconscious and manifest itself in physical and emotional disorders. Thus to let go of something assumes that I was first in possession of it. I can let go of sexual needs only after I have first experienced and accepted them as sexual. If I live in the belief that as a result of celibacy I am missing out on something or that I have lost something, then the focus will not be on letting go, but on deprivation, which is the root of unhappiness, and on the subsequent striving and grasping.

I am assuming here that there is a basic call to celibacy for all Christians, which is a call to freedom and transformation of sexual energy into a higher union of love. If physical union is experienced as mere sexual discharge, it becomes empty, and seemingly reduces vital energy and mental and spiritual powers. The more one is able to let go of sexual needs and transform them into a higher union, the more intense sexual fulfillment seems.

To be able to live a celibate life in a canonical sense demands maturity. One sign of maturity is the ability to endure sexual energies with calm nerves, without irritability, and with the focus not on celibacy but on God. If our primary perception is one of sacrifice, then we will feel irritable and place expectations on God. If control of sex is the focus, then sexual desire will increase and our energies will be directed to a negative sexual fulfillment. To pray to God to help us to control sex adds fuel to the fire. Thus for the celibate, a true desire for God rather than sexual control is the goal.

In a similar way, the call to poverty is a universal call to let go of our grasping for security. Again, it is not the security we relinquish, but the striving. In letting go of the wanting of material things, we come to a new relationship with them. Instead of being an object of desire to be manipulated, or a means of fulfillment, they become an end in themselves. We attain an appreciation of the material world as good and beautiful in itself. We learn the meaning of the Scripture that says God created all things and all that God created was good (Gen. 1:31). Thus we learn to let go of our possessiveness and clinging. We learn to appreciate the world with open hands and receive all as a gift— as grace.

Likewise, in embracing obedience and letting go of our striving for power we attain a new sense of our personal authority. We learn that power does not come from outside forces but from an inner center of richness. Once I attended a retreat during which a priest shared his struggle with alcoholism. During his sharing, I was struck by his power and strength. Others present also made the same observation. By being vulnerable and sharing his weakness, he was strong. Jesus showed his greatest power at the moment of his death—his greatest manifestation of weakness and powerlessness. We give power over ourselves to others because of fear. But if I am not afraid, then others cannot control me. If I have a sense of my own identity and center, I will attain a true authority instead of the pseudopower of direct control.

In the example of the three vows, we let go of our striving for sexual fulfillment, our grasping for material goods, and our desire for control and power. In return we receive a deeper experience of sexuality, a new respect for material realities, and an authentic sense of power. The person who becomes truly celibate also becomes truly sexual. One who is poor in spirit is rich in that the whole world is received as a gift. The person who is obedient is powerful because he or she has the strength to move mountains. However, to let go assumes that we first have experienced our own sexuality and power, and have had attachments to material things. Without such prior experience, letting go is merely that and leads to deprivation, loneliness, and emptiness. We experience doubt, anxiety, confusion, depression, and pain. The tendency is then to turn the pain into self-pity, or to use suffering to play the martyr role and try to manipulate others, or perhaps to give up in the face of pain and want to die. Suffering by itself is no cure. It heals only when we have the right attitude toward it. Growth demands a waiting for, that is, hope.

Judas let go in that he confessed his sins. But all he saw was his own misery, so he committed suicide. Peter also let go by confessing his sins. But he looked outward on the face of Christ and was transformed. To let go means entering the void, the darkness. But it is also a waiting for the light. It is like driving through the fog; when we are in it, it seems endless; but we hope that it will end, that there will be a clearing. When we expect the clearing, however, the fog sometimes seems denser. Thus we must hope against hope. Ultimately it is a waiting for insight—a waiting for God.

Interdependence and Integration

Waiting for insight means letting the darkness reveal the light. Black is experienced as empty—as the void. But rather than being the absence of color, black is the totality of color. The insight we attain is a new relationship to sensations, objects, and persons. We come to a new definition of self and a new integration of heart and mind, body and spirit.

Lastly, we return to share the insight with others. Letting go and waiting for has been a withdrawal into solitude. Now we return to reconnect with community through a sharing of insight. In the discovery of self, we also discover others. Through the experience of pain and vulnerability, we realize that we share the human condition with all people. Thus the process of individuation is also a deepening of communion. The sharing of insight is not merely an intellectual sharing of knowledge, but rather the sharing of living reality. In the sharing, we experience the reality shared. Have you ever experienced a great teacher— one to whom you really felt connected? What was it that gave you that experience? Somehow you realized that this person did not just share ideas and words, but the embodiment of his or her life experience.

In entering into our vulnerability and darkness, we come to a compassion and love for self and others. To experience love is to realize one's unity with all people and all creation. I would suggest that this experience is very different from the reported unity achieved through drugs. I feel suspicious of the insight and wisdom of the teenager who has never struggled with evil and who has not wrestled with God. If one has not known sin, one cannot love. I cannot say that I truly love God if I cannot at the same time acknowledge and experience my own sinfulness.

Conclusion

Thus in the human journey, we are challenged with four stages of growth: needs fulfillment, and a consequent frustration and disillusionment; letting go and waiting for; insight; and interdependence and integration. Happiness is living in congruence with one's stage of development.

There is a story told of a spiritual master who had two disciples. The first disciple crossed the river in a boat. While aboard, he overheard his companions criticizing his master, calling him a fraud and hypocrite. The disciple became furious and threatened to sink the boat. When the disciple later reported to his master what had happened, his master rebuked him and taught him to resist and turn the other cheek. On another occasion, the second disciple was crossing the river. Again his companions were criticizing his master and spreading false rumors about him. Although distressed, the disciple remained silent, feeling there was nothing he could do about it. Besides, he argued, they do not know what they are talking about. When he reported the incident to his master, the master reproved him for allowing such slander in his presence.

The first disciple already knew how to resist people and needed to learn nonviolence. The second disciple acted out of cowardice and needed to learn to be assertive.[6] Happiness means first trying to achieve fulfillment of basic needs. When that goal has been attained, then happiness involves a letting go and waiting for. Happiness, then, is fidelity to my own process, accepting myself at my present developmental stage.

However, if happiness itself is the goal of our struggle, it will elude us. We must let go of happiness itself. If we let go because we believe we will then attain happiness, we have not really let go, but simply reinforced our striving and grasping. Letting go is not a linear process, but a lifelong task. Nonattachment to some persons suggests indifference, laziness, or fatalism. Actually, nonattachment is the opposite of indifference. When we are involved in the exercise of power, or sexuality, or with material realities, we are intensely involved, but we are also able to be detached at a moment's notice. During intense involvement we also experience God and a happiness that remains incomplete.

In summary, to be able to let go of our grasping and striving for security, sexual fulfillment, and power, we need first to experience security, sexuality, and power. In the process, we become disillusioned and frustrated. We realize that our needs can never be totally satisfied. Thus we become able to let go of the wanting and enter into the emptiness and the "not having." In that process, we achieve insight and are led on a journey toward wholeness. The insight reached is a new relationship to

---

6. Swami Prabhavananda, *The Sermon on the Mount According to Vedanta* (New York: Mentor Books, 1972), pp. 64-65.

desire, and a new existential understanding of security, sexuality, and power. Finally, we rediscover others and enter more fully into communion with all people and creation, and in that process, with God. We have thus moved on the physical level from the constraints of a bodily armor that tenses our muscles and blocks pleasure to a joy that is manifest in an increased intensity in the experience of all our senses. The body is still able to defend against real threat, but at the same time, an underlying trust enables us to let go of our armor.

Cognitively we have moved from a quest for certitude to a quest for understanding. Previously we had looked for absolutes. Everything was black and white. Now we come to know the gray. Our lives are filled with uncertainty, but we have also learned to tolerate uncertainty and to be comfortable with ambiguity.

On the interpersonal level, we enter into relationships that are nonpossessive, yet warm, caring, and interdependent. At the same time we are autonomous and interconnected.

Happiness is thus fidelity to one's process—to being led by God, who takes us step by step. Once Jesus was visiting Jericho, where he met the chief tax collector, Zacchaeus. Zacchaeus was a public sinner, one who conspired with the colonizing enemy, Rome, and oppressed his own people through enforcing a tax system that was perceived as unjust and oppressive. Zacchaeus climbed a sycamore tree so as to be able to see Jesus. Jesus acknowledged him and invited himself to dinner—one of the most intimate gestures a Jew could make. In this story we see the way God leads. He befriended Zacchaeus as he was and did not demand that he first give up his sinful ways. Jesus' love transformed Zacchaeus, who then could let go of his cheating and fraudulent ways (Luke 19:1-10). When we befriend our dark side, change becomes possible, and we realize happiness is to be discovered in the valley and in sin itself.

O happy fault!